Practice the HS

High School Placement Test
Practice Test Questions

Published by

Complete TEST Preparation Inc.

Copyright © 2013 by Complete Test Preparation Inc. ALL RIGHTS RESERVED. No part of this book may be reproduced or transferred in any form or by any means, graphic, electronic, or mechanical, including photocopying, recording, web distribution, taping, or by any information storage retrieval system, without the written permission of the author.

Notice: Complete Test Preparation Inc. makes every reasonable effort to obtain from reliable sources accurate, complete, and timely information about the tests covered in this book. Nevertheless, changes can be made in the tests or the administration of the tests at any time and Complete Test Preparation Inc. makes no representation or warranty, either expressed or implied as to the accuracy, timeliness, or completeness of the information contained in this book. Complete Test Preparation Inc. makes no representations or warranties of any kind, express or implied, about the completeness, accuracy, reliability, suitability or availability with respect to the information contained in this document for any purpose. Any reliance you place on such information is therefore strictly at your own risk.

The author(s) shall not be liable for any loss incurred as a consequence of the use and application, directly or indirectly, of any information presented in this work. Sold with the understanding, the author(s) is not engaged in rendering professional services or advice. If advice or expert assistance is required, the services of a competent professional should be sought.

The company, product and service names used in this publication are for identification purposes only. All trademarks and registered trademarks are the property of their respective owners. Complete Test Preparation Inc. is not affiliated with any educational institution.

HSPT® and the High School Placement Test are registered trademarks of Scholastic Testing Service, Inc., who are not involved in the production of, and do not endorse this publication.

Version 6.6 July 2016

We strongly recommend that students check with exam providers for up-to-date information regarding test content.

ISBN-13: 978-1927358672
ISBN-10: 1927358671

Published by
Complete Test Preparation Inc.
Victoria BC Canada

Visit us on the web at http://www.test-preparation.ca
Printed in the USA

About Complete Test Preparation Inc.

Complete Test Preparation Inc. has been publishing high quality study materials since 2005. Thousands of students visit our websites every year, and thousands of students, teachers and parents all over the world have purchased our teaching materials, curriculum, study guides and practice tests.

Complete Test Preparation Inc. is committed to providing students with the best study materials and practice tests available on the market. Members of our team combine years of teaching experience, with experienced writers and editors, all with advanced degrees.

Contents

6   **Getting Started**
The HSPT® Study Plan   7
Making a Study Schedule   8

12   **Practice Test Questions Set 1**
Answer Key   93

123   **Practice Test Questions Set 2**
Answer Key   202

230   **Conclusion**

231   **HSPT Test Strategy Special Offer**

Feedback

We welcome your feedback. Email us at feedback@test-preparation.ca with your comments and suggestions. We carefully review all suggestions and often incorporate reader suggestions into upcoming versions. As a Print on Demand Publisher, we update our products frequently.

Find us on Facebook

WWW.FACEBOOK.COM/CompleteTestPreparation

Getting Started

CONGRATULATIONS! By deciding to take the High School Placement Test (HSPT®), you have taken the first step toward a great future! Of course, there is no point in taking this important examination unless you intend to do your very best in order to earn the highest grade you possibly can. That means getting yourself organized and discovering the best approaches, methods and strategies to master the material. Yes, that will require real effort and dedication on your part but if you are willing to focus your energy and devote the study time necessary, before you know it you will be on you way to a brighter future!

We know that taking on a new endeavour can be a little scary, and it is easy to feel unsure of where to begin. That's where we come in. This study guide is designed to help you improve your test-taking skills, show you a few tricks of the trade and increase both your competency and confidence.

The High School Placement Test

The HSPT® exam is composed of five sections, verbal skills, quantitative skills, reading, mathematics and language skills. The verbal skills section consists of analogies, synonyms and antonyms, logic and verbal classification. The quantitative skills section consists of number series, geometric and non geometric comparisons, and basic math. The reading section consists of quantitative skills and vocabulary questions. The mathematics section consists of problem solving questions or word problems. The language skills section consists of punctuation and capitalization, English usage, spelling and composition.

While we seek to make our guide as comprehensive as possible, it is important to note that like all exams, the HSPT® Exam might be adjusted at some future point. New material might be added, or content that is no longer relevant or applicable might be removed. It is always a good idea to give the materials you receive when you register to take the HSPT® a careful review.

The HSPT® Study Plan

Now that you have made the decision to take the HSPT®, it is time to get started. Before you do another thing, you will need to figure out a plan of attack. The very best study tip is to start early! The longer the time period you devote to regular study practice, the more likely you will be to retain the material and be able to access it quickly. If you thought that 1x20 is the same as 2x10, guess what? It really is not, when it comes to study time. Reviewing material for just an hour per day over the course of 20 days is far better than studying for two hours a day for only 10 days. The more often you revisit a particular piece of information, the better you will know it. Not only will your grasp and understanding be better, but your ability to reach into your brain and quickly and efficiently pull out the tidbit you need, will be greatly enhanced as well.

The great Chinese scholar and philosopher Confucius believed that true knowledge could be defined as knowing both what you know and what you do not know. The first step in preparing for the HSPT® is to assess your strengths and weaknesses. You may already have an idea of what you know and what you do not know, but evaluating yourself using our Self- Assessment modules for each of the three areas, Math, Writing and Quantitative skills, will clarify the details.

Making a Study Schedule

To make your study time most productive you will need to develop a study plan. The purpose of the plan is to organize all the bits of pieces of information in such a way that you will not feel overwhelmed. Rome was not built in a day, and learning everything you will need to know in order to pass the HSPT® is going to take time, too. Arranging the material you need to learn into manageable chunks is the best way to go. Each study session should make you feel as though you have succeeded in accomplishing your goal, and your goal is simply to learn what you planned to learn during that particular session. Try to organize the content in such a way that each study session builds upon previous ones. That way, you will retain the information, be better able to access it, and review the previous bits and pieces at the same time.

Self-assessment

The Best Study Tip! The very best study tip is to start early! The longer you study regularly, the more you will retain and 'learn' the material. Studying for 1 hour per day for 20 days is far better than studying for 2 hours for 10 days.

What don't you know?

The first step is to assess your strengths and weaknesses. You may already have an idea of where your weaknesses are, or you can take our Self-assessment modules for each of the areas, Math, English, Science and Quantitative skills.

Exam Component	Rate 1 to 5
Verbal Skills	
Verbal Analogies	
Synonyms	
Logic	
Verbal Classifications	
Antonyms	
Quantitative Skills	
Number Series	
Geometric Comparison	
Non-geometric Comparison	
Number Manipulation	
Quantitative skills	
Vocabulary	
Mathematics	
Mathematical Concepts	
Problem-Solving	
Language Skills	
Punctuation and Capitalization	
Usage	
Spelling	

Making a Study Schedule

The key to making a study plan is to divide the material you need to learn into manageable sized pieces and learn it, while at the same time reviewing the material that you already know.

Using the table above, any scores of 3 or below, you need to spend time learning, going over and practicing this subject area. A score of 4 means you need to review the material, but you don't have to spend time re-learning. A score of 5 and you are OK with just an occasional review before the exam.
A score of 0 or 1 means you really need to work on this should allocate the most time and the highest priority. Some students prefer a 5-day plan and others a 10-day plan. It also depends on how much time you have until the exam.
Here is an example of a 5-day plan based on an example from the table above:

Verbal Analogies: 1- Study 1 hour everyday – review on last day
Decimals: 3 - Study 1 hour for 2 days then ½ hour a day, then review
Problem Solving: 4 - Review every second day
Geometric Comparison: 2 - Study 1 hour first day – then ½ hour everyday
Quantitative skills: 5 - Review for ½ hour every other day
Usage:5 - Review for ½ hour every other day

Using this example, Spelling and Grammar are good and only need occasional review. Geometric Comparison is good and needs 'some' review. Vocabulary needs a bit of work, Word Problems need a lot of work and Verbal Analogies are very weak and need the most time. Based on this, here is a sample study plan:

Day	Subject	Time
Monday		
Study	Verbal Analogies	1 hour
Study	Word Problems	1 hour
½ hour break		
Study	Vocabulary	1 hour
Review	Reading Comp.	½ hour
Tuesday		
Study	Verbal Analogies	1 hour
Study	Word Problems	½ hour
½ hour break		
Study	Vocabulary	½ hour

Review	Geometric Comparisons	½ hour
Review	Usage	½ hour
Wednesday		
Study	Verbal Analogies	1 hour
Study	Word Problems	½ hour
½ hour break		
Study	Vocabulary	½ hour
Review	Reading Comp.	½ hour
Thursday		
Study	Verbal Analogies	½ hour
Study	Word Problems	½ hour
Review	Vocabulary	½ hour
½ hour break		
Review	Usage	½ hour
Review	Geometric Comparisons	½ hour
Friday		
Review	Verbal Analogies	½ hour
Review	Word Problems	½ hour
Review	Vocabulary	½ hour
½ hour break		
Review	Geometric Comparisons	½ hour
Review	Usage	½ hour

Using this example, adapt the study plan to your own schedule. This schedule assumes 2 ½ - 3 hours available to study everyday for a 5 day period.

First, write out what you need to study and how much. Next figure out how many days you have before the test. Note, do NOT study on the last day before the test. On the last day before the test, you won't learn anything and will probably only confuse yourself.

Make a table with the days before the test and the number of hours you have available to study each day. We suggest working with 1 hour and ½ hour time slots.

Start filling in the blanks, with the subjects you need to study the most getting the most time and the most regular time slots (i.e. everyday) and the subjects that you know getting the least time (e.g. ½ hour every other day, or every 3rd day).

Tips for making a schedule

Once you make a schedule, stick with it! Make your study sessions reasonable. If you make a study schedule and don't stick with it, you set yourself up for failure. Instead, schedule study sessions that are a bit shorter and set yourself up for success! Make sure your study sessions are do-able. Studying is hard work but after you pass, you can party and take a break!

Schedule breaks. Breaks are just as important as study time. Work out a rotation of studying and breaks that works for you.

Build up study time. If you find it hard to sit still and study for 1 hour straight through, build up to it. Start with 20 minutes, and then take a break. Once you get used to 20-minute study sessions, increase the time to 30 minutes. Gradually work you way up to 1 hour.

40 minutes to 1 hour is optimal. Studying for longer than this is tiring and not productive. Studying for shorter isn't long enough to be productive.

Studying Math. Studying Math is different from studying other subjects because you use a different part of your brain. The best way to study math is to practice everyday. This will train your mind to think in a mathematical way. If you miss a day or days, the mathematical mind-set is gone and you have to start all over again to build it up.

Study and practice math everyday for at least 5 days before the exam.

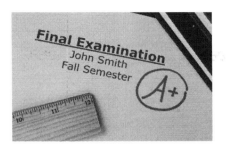

Practice Test Questions Set 1

THE QUESTIONS BELOW ARE NOT THE SAME AS YOU WILL FIND ON THE HSPT® - THAT WOULD BE TOO EASY! And nobody knows what the questions will be and they change all the time. Below are general questions that cover the same subject areas as the HSPT®. So, while the format and exact wording of the questions may differ slightly, and change from year to year, if you can answer the questions below, you will have no problem with the HSPT®.

For the best results, take these practice test questions as if it were the real exam. Set aside time when you will not be disturbed, and a location that is quiet and free of distractions. Read the instructions carefully, read each question carefully, and answer to the best of your ability.
Use the bubble answer sheets provided. When you have completed the practice questions, check your answer against the Answer Key and read the explanation provided.

Do not attempt more than one set of practice test questions in one day. After completing the first practice test, wait two or three days before attempting the second set of questions.

Section I – Verbal Skills
Questions: 60
Time: 16 Minutes

Section II – Quantitative Skills
Questions: 50
Time: 30 Minutes

Section III – Reading & Vocabulary
Questions: 60
Time: 25 Minutes

Section IV – Math
Questions: 60
Time: 45 Minutes

Section V – Language
Questions: 60
Time: 25 Minutes

Verbal Skills Answer Sheet

1. Ⓐ Ⓑ Ⓒ Ⓓ   21. Ⓐ Ⓑ Ⓒ Ⓓ   41. Ⓐ Ⓑ Ⓒ Ⓓ

2. Ⓐ Ⓑ Ⓒ Ⓓ   22. Ⓐ Ⓑ Ⓒ Ⓓ   42. Ⓐ Ⓑ Ⓒ Ⓓ

3. Ⓐ Ⓑ Ⓒ Ⓓ   23. Ⓐ Ⓑ Ⓒ Ⓓ   43. Ⓐ Ⓑ Ⓒ Ⓓ

4. Ⓐ Ⓑ Ⓒ Ⓓ   24. Ⓐ Ⓑ Ⓒ Ⓓ   44. Ⓐ Ⓑ Ⓒ Ⓓ

5. Ⓐ Ⓑ Ⓒ Ⓓ   25. Ⓐ Ⓑ Ⓒ Ⓓ   45. Ⓐ Ⓑ Ⓒ Ⓓ

6. Ⓐ Ⓑ Ⓒ Ⓓ   26. Ⓐ Ⓑ Ⓒ Ⓓ   46. Ⓐ Ⓑ Ⓒ Ⓓ

7. Ⓐ Ⓑ Ⓒ Ⓓ   27. Ⓐ Ⓑ Ⓒ Ⓓ   47. Ⓐ Ⓑ Ⓒ Ⓓ

8. Ⓐ Ⓑ Ⓒ Ⓓ   28. Ⓐ Ⓑ Ⓒ Ⓓ   48. Ⓐ Ⓑ Ⓒ Ⓓ

9. Ⓐ Ⓑ Ⓒ Ⓓ   29. Ⓐ Ⓑ Ⓒ Ⓓ   49. Ⓐ Ⓑ Ⓒ Ⓓ

10. Ⓐ Ⓑ Ⓒ Ⓓ   30. Ⓐ Ⓑ Ⓒ Ⓓ   50. Ⓐ Ⓑ Ⓒ Ⓓ

11. Ⓐ Ⓑ Ⓒ Ⓓ   31. Ⓐ Ⓑ Ⓒ Ⓓ   51. Ⓐ Ⓑ Ⓒ Ⓓ

12. Ⓐ Ⓑ Ⓒ Ⓓ   32. Ⓐ Ⓑ Ⓒ Ⓓ   52. Ⓐ Ⓑ Ⓒ Ⓓ

13. Ⓐ Ⓑ Ⓒ Ⓓ   33. Ⓐ Ⓑ Ⓒ Ⓓ   53. Ⓐ Ⓑ Ⓒ Ⓓ

14. Ⓐ Ⓑ Ⓒ Ⓓ   34. Ⓐ Ⓑ Ⓒ Ⓓ   54. Ⓐ Ⓑ Ⓒ Ⓓ

15. Ⓐ Ⓑ Ⓒ Ⓓ   35. Ⓐ Ⓑ Ⓒ Ⓓ   55. Ⓐ Ⓑ Ⓒ Ⓓ

16. Ⓐ Ⓑ Ⓒ Ⓓ   36. Ⓐ Ⓑ Ⓒ Ⓓ   56. Ⓐ Ⓑ Ⓒ Ⓓ

17. Ⓐ Ⓑ Ⓒ Ⓓ   37. Ⓐ Ⓑ Ⓒ Ⓓ   57. Ⓐ Ⓑ Ⓒ Ⓓ

18. Ⓐ Ⓑ Ⓒ Ⓓ   38. Ⓐ Ⓑ Ⓒ Ⓓ   58. Ⓐ Ⓑ Ⓒ Ⓓ

19. Ⓐ Ⓑ Ⓒ Ⓓ   39. Ⓐ Ⓑ Ⓒ Ⓓ   59. Ⓐ Ⓑ Ⓒ Ⓓ

20. Ⓐ Ⓑ Ⓒ Ⓓ   40. Ⓐ Ⓑ Ⓒ Ⓓ   60. Ⓐ Ⓑ Ⓒ Ⓓ

Quantitative Skills Answer Sheet

1. (A) (B) (C) (D)
2. (A) (B) (C) (D)
3. (A) (B) (C) (D)
4. (A) (B) (C) (D)
5. (A) (B) (C) (D)
6. (A) (B) (C) (D)
7. (A) (B) (C) (D)
8. (A) (B) (C) (D)
9. (A) (B) (C) (D)
10. (A) (B) (C) (D)
11. (A) (B) (C) (D)
12. (A) (B) (C) (D)
13. (A) (B) (C) (D)
14. (A) (B) (C) (D)
15. (A) (B) (C) (D)
16. (A) (B) (C) (D)
17. (A) (B) (C) (D)

18. (A) (B) (C) (D)
19. (A) (B) (C) (D)
20. (A) (B) (C) (D)
21. (A) (B) (C) (D)
22. (A) (B) (C) (D)
23. (A) (B) (C) (D)
24. (A) (B) (C) (D)
25. (A) (B) (C) (D)
26. (A) (B) (C) (D)
27. (A) (B) (C) (D)
28. (A) (B) (C) (D)
29. (A) (B) (C) (D)
30. (A) (B) (C) (D)
31. (A) (B) (C) (D)
32. (A) (B) (C) (D)
33. (A) (B) (C) (D)
34. (A) (B) (C) (D)

35. (A) (B) (C) (D)
36. (A) (B) (C) (D)
37. (A) (B) (C) (D)
38. (A) (B) (C) (D)
39. (A) (B) (C) (D)
40. (A) (B) (C) (D)
41. (A) (B) (C) (D)
42. (A) (B) (C) (D)
43. (A) (B) (C) (D)
44. (A) (B) (C) (D)
45. (A) (B) (C) (D)
46. (A) (B) (C) (D)
47. (A) (B) (C) (D)
48. (A) (B) (C) (D)
49. (A) (B) (C) (D)
50. (A) (B) (C) (D)

Reading Comprehension and Vocabulary Answer Sheet

1. (A) (B) (C) (D)   21. (A) (B) (C) (D)   41. (A) (B) (C) (D)

2. (A) (B) (C) (D)   22. (A) (B) (C) (D)   42. (A) (B) (C) (D)

3. (A) (B) (C) (D)   23. (A) (B) (C) (D)   43. (A) (B) (C) (D)

4. (A) (B) (C) (D)   24. (A) (B) (C) (D)   44. (A) (B) (C) (D)

5. (A) (B) (C) (D)   25. (A) (B) (C) (D)   45. (A) (B) (C) (D)

6. (A) (B) (C) (D)   26. (A) (B) (C) (D)   46. (A) (B) (C) (D)

7. (A) (B) (C) (D)   27. (A) (B) (C) (D)   47. (A) (B) (C) (D)

8. (A) (B) (C) (D)   28. (A) (B) (C) (D)   48. (A) (B) (C) (D)

9. (A) (B) (C) (D)   29. (A) (B) (C) (D)   49. (A) (B) (C) (D)

10. (A) (B) (C) (D)   30. (A) (B) (C) (D)   50. (A) (B) (C) (D)

11. (A) (B) (C) (D)   31. (A) (B) (C) (D)   51. (A) (B) (C) (D)

12. (A) (B) (C) (D)   32. (A) (B) (C) (D)   52. (A) (B) (C) (D)

13. (A) (B) (C) (D)   33. (A) (B) (C) (D)   53. (A) (B) (C) (D)

14. (A) (B) (C) (D)   34. (A) (B) (C) (D)   54. (A) (B) (C) (D)

15. (A) (B) (C) (D)   35. (A) (B) (C) (D)   55. (A) (B) (C) (D)

16. (A) (B) (C) (D)   36. (A) (B) (C) (D)   56. (A) (B) (C) (D)

17. (A) (B) (C) (D)   37. (A) (B) (C) (D)   57. (A) (B) (C) (D)

18. (A) (B) (C) (D)   38. (A) (B) (C) (D)   58. (A) (B) (C) (D)

19. (A) (B) (C) (D)   39. (A) (B) (C) (D)   59. (A) (B) (C) (D)

20. (A) (B) (C) (D)   40. (A) (B) (C) (D)   60. (A) (B) (C) (D)

Mathematics Answer Sheet

1. A B C D   21. A B C D   41. A B C D
2. A B C D   22. A B C D   42. A B C D
3. A B C D   23. A B C D   43. A B C D
4. A B C D   24. A B C D   44. A B C D
5. A B C D   25. A B C D   45. A B C D
6. A B C D   26. A B C D   46. A B C D
7. A B C D   27. A B C D   47. A B C D
8. A B C D   28. A B C D   48. A B C D
9. A B C D   29. A B C D   49. A B C D
10. A B C D   30. A B C D   50. A B C D
11. A B C D   31. A B C D   51. A B C D
12. A B C D   32. A B C D   52. A B C D
13. A B C D   33. A B C D   53. A B C D
14. A B C D   34. A B C D   54. A B C D
15. A B C D   35. A B C D   55. A B C D
16. A B C D   36. A B C D   56. A B C D
17. A B C D   37. A B C D   57. A B C D
18. A B C D   38. A B C D   58. A B C D
19. A B C D   39. A B C D   59. A B C D
20. A B C D   40. A B C D   60. A B C D

Language Arts Answer Sheet

1. (A) (B) (C) (D)   21. (A) (B) (C) (D)   41. (A) (B) (C) (D)

2. (A) (B) (C) (D)   22. (A) (B) (C) (D)   42. (A) (B) (C) (D)

3. (A) (B) (C) (D)   23. (A) (B) (C) (D)   43. (A) (B) (C) (D)

4. (A) (B) (C) (D)   24. (A) (B) (C) (D)   44. (A) (B) (C) (D)

5. (A) (B) (C) (D)   25. (A) (B) (C) (D)   45. (A) (B) (C) (D)

6. (A) (B) (C) (D)   26. (A) (B) (C) (D)   46. (A) (B) (C) (D)

7. (A) (B) (C) (D)   27. (A) (B) (C) (D)   47. (A) (B) (C) (D)

8. (A) (B) (C) (D)   28. (A) (B) (C) (D)   48. (A) (B) (C) (D)

9. (A) (B) (C) (D)   29. (A) (B) (C) (D)   49. (A) (B) (C) (D)

10. (A) (B) (C) (D)   30. (A) (B) (C) (D)   50. (A) (B) (C) (D)

11. (A) (B) (C) (D)   31. (A) (B) (C) (D)   51. (A) (B) (C) (D)

12. (A) (B) (C) (D)   32. (A) (B) (C) (D)   52. (A) (B) (C) (D)

13. (A) (B) (C) (D)   33. (A) (B) (C) (D)   53. (A) (B) (C) (D)

14. (A) (B) (C) (D)   34. (A) (B) (C) (D)   54. (A) (B) (C) (D)

15. (A) (B) (C) (D)   35. (A) (B) (C) (D)   55. (A) (B) (C) (D)

16. (A) (B) (C) (D)   36. (A) (B) (C) (D)   56. (A) (B) (C) (D)

17. (A) (B) (C) (D)   37. (A) (B) (C) (D)   57. (A) (B) (C) (D)

18. (A) (B) (C) (D)   38. (A) (B) (C) (D)   58. (A) (B) (C) (D)

19. (A) (B) (C) (D)   39. (A) (B) (C) (D)   59. (A) (B) (C) (D)

20. (A) (B) (C) (D)   40. (A) (B) (C) (D)   60. (A) (B) (C) (D)

Section I – Verbal Skills

Choose the option with the same relationship.

1. Lawyer : Trial

    a. Plumber : Pipe

    b. Businessman : Secretary

    c. Doctor : Operation

    d. Hairdresser : Blow Dryer

2. Fat : Eat

    a. Swim : Water

    b. Live : Breathe

    c. Walk : Run

    d. Sing : Song

3. Dog : Canine

    a. Elephant : Large

    b. Tree : Flower

    c. Cat : Mouse

    d. Porpoise : Mammal

4. Turntable : MP3 player

    a. Horse Drawn Carriage : Vehicle

    b. Radio : Telephone

    c. Calculator : Computer

    d. Documentary : Movie

5. Cub : Bear

    a. Piano : Orchestra

    b. Puppy : Dog

    c. Cat : Kitten

    d. Eagle : Predator

6. Medicine : Illness

a. Law : Anarchy

b. Hunger : Thirst

c. Etiquette : Discipline

d. Stimulant : Sensitivity

7. Gold : Metal

a. Carnivorous : Veterinarian

b. Surgeon : Doctor

c. Secretary : Lawyer

d. Potato : Farmer

8. Melt : Liquid :: Freeze : _____

a. Ice

b. Condense

c. Solid

d. Steam

9. Clock : Time :: Thermometer : _____

a. Heat

b. Radiation

c. Energy

d. Temperature

10. Car : Garage :: Plane : _____

a. Depot

b. Port

c. Hanger

d. Harbor

11. Select the synonym of peculiar.

    a. New

    b. Strange

    c. Imaginative

    d. Funny

12. Select the synonym of tippet.

    a. Necktie

    b. Shawl

    c. Sweater

    d. Blouse

13. Select the synonym of vivid.

    a. Glamorous

    b. Bountiful

    c. Varied

    d. Brilliant

14. Select the synonym of semblance.

    a. Personality

    b. Image

    c. Attitude

    d. ambition

15. Select the synonym of impregnable.

    a. Unconquerable

    b. Impossible

    c. Unlimited

    d. Imperfect

16. Choose the synonym pair.

    a. Jargon and Slang

    b. Slander and Plagiarism

    c. Devotion and Devout

    d. Current and Outdated

17. Choose the synonym pair.

    a. Render and Give

    b. Recognition and Cognizant

    c. Stem and Root

    d. Adjust and Redo

18. Choose the synonym pair.

    a. Private and Public

    b. Intrusive and Invasive

    c. Mysterious and Unknown

    d. Common and Unique

19. Choose the synonym pair.

    a. Renowned and Popular

    b. Guard and Safe

    c. Aggressive and Shy

    d. Curtail and Avoid

20. Choose the synonym pair.

    a. Brevity and Ambiguous

    b. Fury and Light-hearted

    c. Incoherent and Jumbled

    d. benign and malignant

21. Choose the synonym pair.

    a. Congenial and Pleasant

    b. Distort and Similar

    c. Valuable and Rich

    d. Asset and Liability

22. Choose the synonym pair.

    a. Circumstance and Plan

    b. Negotiate and Scheme

    c. Ardent and Whimsical

    d. Plight and Situation

23. Choose the synonym pair.

    a. Berate and Criticize

    b. Unspoken and Unknown

    c. Tenet and Favor

    d. Turf and Seashore

24. Choose the synonym pair.

    a. Adequate and Inadequate

    b. Sate and Satisfy

    c. Sufficient and Lacking

    d. Spectator and Teacher

25. Choose the synonym pair.

    a. Pensive and Alibi

    b. Terminate and End

    c. Plot and Point

    d. Jaded and Honest

26. Which does not belong?

a. abcabc

b. defdef

c. ghihij

d. mnomno

27. Which does not belong?

a. Anguish

b. Distress

c. Despair

d. Pain

28. Which does not belong?

a. DDDdddEEE

b. MMMnnnOOO

c. GGGhhhIII

d. JJJkkkLLL

29. Which does not belong?

a. cde

b. mno

c. stu

d. abc

30. Which does not belong?

a. 446688

b. 224466

c. 336699

d. 446688

31. Which does not belong?

  a. Slant
  b. Lean
  c. Tilt
  d. Incline

32. Which does not belong?

  a. MnOp
  b. AbCD
  c. QrSt
  d. WxYz

33. Which does not belong?

  a. Look
  b. See
  c. Perceive
  d. Surmise

34. Which does not belong?

  a. Count
  b. Number
  c. Add up
  d. List

35. Which does not belong?

  a. Secure
  b. Discard
  c. Throw out
  d. Abandon

36. Which does not belong?

a. Nop

b. Tuv

c. efg

d. Def

37. Which does not belong?

a. Dog

b. Wolf

c. Terrier

d. Cougar

38. Which does not belong?

a. Awkward

b. Graceless

c. Overweight

d. Inept

39. Which does not belong?

a. Smart

b. Great

c. Noteworthy

d. Supreme

40. Which does not belong?

a. Ask

b. Question

c. Query

d. Command

41. Which does not belong?

a. Assume

b. Certain

c. Sure

d. Positive

42. Choose the antonym pair.

a. Dissatisfied and Unsatisfied

b. Disentangle and Acknowledge

c. Discord and Harmony

d. Fruition and Fusion

43. Choose the antonym pair.

a. Late and Later

b. Latter and Former

c. Structure and Organization

d. Latter and Rushed

44. Choose the antonym pair.

a. Belittle and Bemuse

b. Shrunk and Minimal

c. Shrink and Expand

d. Smelly and Odor

45. Choose the antonym pair.

a. Repulsive and Repentant

b. Reluctant and Enthusiastic

c. Prepare and Ready

d. Release and Give

46. Choose the antonym pair.

    a. Sovereign and Autonomy

    b. Disdain and Contempt

    c. Disorder and Disarray

    d. Refute and Agree

47. Choose the antonym pair.

    a. Gentle and Soft

    b. Fragile and Breakable

    c. Vulnerable and Strong

    d. Vain and Tidy

48. Choose the antonym pair.

    a. Daring and Bold

    b. Colossal and Foreign

    c. Awesome and Amazing

    d. Intrepid and Timid

49. Choose the antonym pair.

    a. Liaise and Uncoordinated

    b. Coalesce and Coordinate

    c. Collaborate and Combine

    d. Encourage and Urge

50. Choose the antonym pair.

    a. Ridiculous and Funny

    b. Laughter and Bliss

    c. Famous and Popular

    d. Ridicule and Praise

51. Choose the antonym pair.

    a. Perception and Belief

    b. Fixed and Indefinite

    c. Signal and Symbol

    d. Appearance and Look

52. Select the antonym of flamboyant.

    a. Plain

    b. Colored

    c. Dark

    d. Light

53. Select the antonym of sporadic.

    a. Frequent

    b. Irregular

    c. Regular

    d. Movement

54. Whenever I swim in the ocean I get cold. I went swimming today. I will be getting cold very soon. If the first 2 statements are true, then the third statement is:

True   False   Uncertain

55. Fish can't breathe out of the water. Fish use their gills to breathe. Gills don't work out of water. If the first 2 statements are true, then the third statement is:

True   False   Uncertain

56. I eat steak when I am hungry. I ate steak last night. I was hungry last night. If the first 2 statements are true, then the third statement is:

True   False   Uncertain

57. I read a lot. My favorite author is Herman Melville. I have read all of Herman Melville's books. If the first 2 statements are true, then the third statement is:

True   False   Uncertain

58. All books are very informative. I am reading a book. I will learn something from this book. If the first 2 statements are true, then the third statement is:

True   False   Uncertain

59. Some cats have no tails. All cats are mammals. Some mammals have no tails. If the first 2 statements are true, then the third statement is:

True   False   Uncertain

60. All students carry backpacks. My grandfather carries a backpack. Therefore, my grandfather is a student. If the first 2 statements are true, then the third statement is:

True   False   Uncertain

Section II – Quantitative Skills

1. Consider the following series: 6, 11, 18, 27 ... What number should come next?

    a. 38
    b. 35
    c. 29
    d. 30

2. Consider Box A and the relationship to the numbers in Box B. What is the missing number in Box B?

Box A

6	3
9	5

Box B

36	?
81	25

     a. 49

     b. 51

     c. 9

     d. 12

3. Consider Box A and the relationship to the numbers in Box B. What is the missing number in Box B?

Box A

8	12
5	9

Box B

19	27
13	?

     a. 18

     b. 21

     c. 24

     d. 14

4. Consider the following series: 13, 26, 52, 104. What number should come next?

    a. 208

    b. 106

    c. 200

    d. 400

5. Consider the following series: 32, 26, 20, 14. What number should come next?

    a. 12

    b. 19

    c. 10

    d. 8

6. Consider the following series: 12, 4, 16, ..., 36. What is the missing number?

    a. 18

    b. 22

    c. 20

    d. 30

7. Consider the following series: 3, 9, 27, ..., 243. What is the missing number?

    a. 30

    b. 39

    c. 18

    d. 81

8. Consider the series in row A compared to row B. What is the missing number?

A	5	20	100	3	24
B	20	80	400	12	?

    a. 96

    b. 48

    c. 64

    d. 66

9. Consider the following series: 29, 39, 46, 56, ..., 25. What is the missing number?

    a. 40

    b. 20

    c. 15

    d. 39

10. Consider the following series: L, N, P, R. What letter should come next?

    a. S

    b. T

    c. U

    d. V

11. Consider the following series: M, P, S, ..., Y. What is the missing letter?

    a. V

    b. T

    c. U

    d. X

12. Consider the following series: 14, 21, 28, 35. What number should come next?

    a. 63

    b. 24

    c. 49

    d. 42

13. Consider the following series: 8, 11, 9, 12, 10, 13. What number should come next?

    a. 11

    b. 10

    c. 15

    d. 16

14. Consider the following series: 2, 1, 1/2, 1/4. What number should come next?

    a. 1/3

    b. 1/8

    c. 1/16

    d. 2/8

15. Consider the following series: 17, 23, 29, 35. What 3 numbers should come next?

    a. 41, 47, 54

    b. 42, 47, 53

    c. 40, 45, 50

    d. 41, 47, 53

16. Consider the following series: 11, 15, 20, 26. What 3 numbers should come next?

    a. 31, 37, 42
    b. 33, 41, 50,
    c. 32, 38, 46
    d. 36, 46, 56

17. Consider the following series: 17, 14, 8, -4. What 2 numbers should come next?

    a. -12, -36
    b. -28, -76
    c. -12, -24
    d. -28, -48

18. Consider the following series: -7, -3, 1, 5. What 2 numbers should come next?

    a. 9, 13
    b. 8, 11
    c. -9, 14
    d. 8, 12

19. Examine (A), (B) and (C) and find the best answer.

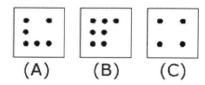

    a. (A) has more dots than (B)
    b. (A) has more than (C)
    c. (A) has more than (B) and (C)
    d. (A) (B) and (C) have an equal number of dots.

Practice Test Questions 1

20. Examine (A), (B) and (C) and find the best answer.

    a. (A) has more dots than (B)
    b. (B) has more than (A)
    c. (A) has more than (B) and (C)
    d. (A) (B) and (C) have an equal number of dots.

21. Examine (A) (B) and (C) and find the best answer.

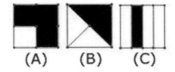

(A)   (B)   (C)

    a. The shaded area in (A) is equal to (B)
    b. The shaded area in (B) is greater than (A)
    c. The shaded area in (A) is less than (C)
    d. The shaded area in (B) is greater than (C)

22. Examine (A) (B) and (C) and find the best answer.

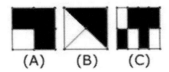

(A)   (B)   (C)

    a. The shaded area in (A) is equal to (C)
    b. The shaded area in (C) is greater than (B)
    c. The shaded area in (A) is greater than (C)
    d. The shaded area in (B) is equal to (C)

23. **Examine (A) (B) and (C) and find the best answer.**

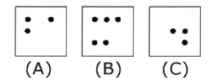

a. The shaded area in (A) is equal to (C)
b. The shaded area in (C) is greater than (B)
c. The shaded area in (A) is greater than (C)
d. The shaded area in (B) is greater than (C)

24. **Examine (A) (B) and find the best answer.**

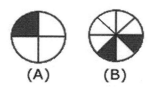

a. The shaded area in (A) is equal to (B)
b. The shaded area in (A) is greater than (B)
c. The shaded area in (B) is less than (A)

25. Examine (A) (B) and (C) and find the best answer.

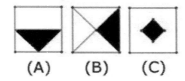

a. The shaded area in (A) is equal to (C)
b. The shaded area in (C) is greater than (B)
c. The shaded area in (A) is greater than (C)
d. The shaded area in (B) is equal to (C)

26. Examine (A) (B) and (C) and find the best answer.

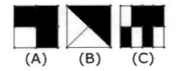

a. The shaded area in (A) is equal to (C)
b. The shaded area in (B) is greater than (C)
c. The shaded area in (A) is greater than (C)
d. The shaded area in (B) is equal to (C)

27. Examine (A) (B) and (C) and find the best answer.

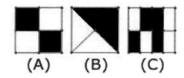

a. The shaded area in (A) is equal to (C)
b. The shaded area in (C) is greater than (B)
c. The shaded area in (A) is greater than (C)
d. The shaded area in (B) is less than (C)

28. Examine the following and find the best answer.

1. (4 X 7) - 12
2. (2 X 14) + 5
3. (3 X 10) – 8

    a. 1 < 2 < 3
    b. 1 < 2 > 3
    c. 2 > 3 < 1
    d. 3 > 2 < 1

29. Examine the following and find the best answer.

1. (8 X 2) X (2 X 3)
2. (4 X 8) + (2 X 6)
3. (3 X 4) X (9 - 2)
4. (3 X 7) - (2 X 6)

    a. 1 < 3 < 4
    b. 1 > 4 < 3
    c. 2 > 1 > 3
    d. 4 < 1 < 3

30. Examine the following and find the best answer.

1. 12 + (15 - 4)
2. 9 + (24 - 2)
3. 2 + (19 + 7)
4. 15 + (26 - 19)

    a. 1 < 3 < 4

    b. 1 < 4 < 3

    c. 2 > 1 < 3

    d. 4 > 1 < 3

31. Examine the following and find the best answer.

1. (23 - 7) * 2
2. (9 + 12) / 7
3. (13 - 7) X 2
4. (17 + 4) + 1

    a. 2 is the smallest

    b. 4 is the largest

    c. 1 is the smallest

    d. None of the Above

32. Examine the following and find the best answer.

1. 1 + (6 * 7)
2. 7 - 22
3. 9 + (13 X 2)
4. 6 * (5 + 2)

    a. 3 and 4 are greater than 1

    b. 3 and 2 are greater than 1

    c. 3 is less than 2

    d. None of the Above

33. Examine the following and find the best answer.

1. 19 + (4 X 5)
2. 13 - (4 + 6)
3. 7 + (3 X 7)

    a. 1 > 2 < 3
    b. 2 > 3 < 1
    c. 2 < 3 > 1
    d. 1 < 2 < 3

34. Examine the following and find the best answer.

1. 18 + 7
2. 4 X 8
3. 3 X 5
4. 2 X 10

    a. (#2 - #4) > #1
    b. (#4 - #3) > #2
    c. (#2 - #1) < #3
    d. (#1 + #2) > #4

35. Examine the following and find the best answer.

1. (6 X 3) X (3 X 4)
2. (4 X 5) + (3 X 6)
3. (3 X 4) X (5 - 2)

    a. 3 is the largest
    b. 1 is less than 2
    c. 3 is greater than 1
    d. None of the Above

36. What is the smallest value?

    a. 4 % of 4
    b. 5 % of 5
    c. 0.3% of 12
    d. 1/5 of 100

Practice Test Questions 1

37. What is 8 more than 2/5 of 20?

    a. 10
    b. 12
    c. 16
    d. 8

38. What is 6 more than 50% of 50?

    a. 31
    b. 41
    c. 25
    d. 26

39. What number subtracted from 100 leaves 7 more than 3/4 of 40?

    a. 50
    b. 63
    c. 47
    d. 75

40. What number divided by 5 is 1/4 of 100?

    a. 125
    b. 150
    c. 75
    d. 225

41. 1/5 of what number is 5 times 10?

    a. 150
    b. 200
    c. 250
    d. 100

42. What number multiplied by 5 is 10 less than 52?

    a. 8.4

    b. 10.24

    c. 20

    d. 22.5

43. What number subtracted from 25 is 1/5 of 20?

    a. 125

    b. 150

    c. 50

    d. 21

44. What number is 15 less than 3/5 of 40?

    a. 42

    b. 17

    c. 9

    d. 18

45. What number is 10 times 1/2 of 60?

    a. 100

    b. 300

    c. 250

    d. 75

46. 1/4 of what number is 8 times 10?

    a. 150

    b. 200

    c. 320

    d. 100

47. 1/2 of what number is 4 X 15

    a. 120

    b. 40

    c. 50

    d. 60

48. 5 X 60 = 1/3 of what number?

    a. 50

    b. 900

    c. 150

    d. 200

49. 1/4 of what number added to 20 is 4 times 8?

    a. 10

    b. 8

    c. 6

    d. 48

50. What number subtracted from 500 leaves 10 more than 3/4 of 100?

    a. 600

    b. 415

    c. 525

    d. 400

Section III - Reading

Questions 1 – 4 refer to the following passage.

Passage 1 - Infectious Disease

An infectious disease is a clinically evident illness resulting from the presence of pathogenic agents, such as viruses, bacteria, fungi, protozoa, multi-cellular parasites, and unusual proteins known as prions. Infectious pathologies are also called communicable diseases or transmissible diseases, due to their potential of transmission from one person or species to another by a replicating agent (as opposed to a toxin).

Transmission of an infectious disease can occur in many different ways. Physical contact, liquids, food, body fluids, contaminated objects, and airborne inhalation can all transmit infecting agents.

Transmissible diseases that occur through contact with an ill person, or objects touched by them, are especially infective, and are sometimes called contagious diseases. Communicable diseases that require a more specialized route of infection, such as through blood or needle transmission, or sexual transmission, are usually not regarded as contagious.

The term infectivity describes the ability of an organism to enter, survive and multiply in the host, while the infectiousness of a disease shows the comparative ease with which the disease is transmitted. An infection however, is not synonymous with an infectious disease, as an infection may not cause important clinical symptoms. [3]

1. What can we infer from the first paragraph in this passage?

    a. Sickness from a toxin can be easily transmitted from one person to another.

    b. Sickness from an infectious disease can be easily transmitted from one person to another.

    c. Few sicknesses are transmitted from one person to another.

    d. Infectious diseases are easily treated.

2. What are two other names for infections' pathologies?

    a. Communicable diseases or transmissible diseases

    b. Communicable diseases or terminal diseases

    c. Transmissible diseases or preventable diseases

d. Communicative diseases or unstable diseases

3. What does infectivity describe?

a. The inability of an organism to multiply in the host.

b. The inability of an organism to reproduce.

c. The ability of an organism to enter, survive and multiply in the host.

d. The ability of an organism to reproduce in the host.

4. How do we know an infection is not synonymous with an infectious disease?

a. Because an infectious disease destroys infections with enough time.

b. Because an infection may not cause important clinical symptoms or impair host function.

c. We do not. The two are synonymous.

d. Because an infection is too fatal to be an infectious disease.

Questions 5 – 8 refer to the following passage.

Passage 2 - Viruses

A virus (from the Latin virus meaning toxin or poison) is a small infectious agent that can replicate only inside the living cells of other organisms. Most viruses are too small to be seen directly with a microscope. Viruses infect all types of organisms, from animals and plants to bacteria and single-celled organisms.

Unlike prions and viroids, viruses consist of two or three parts: all viruses have genes made from either DNA or RNA, all have a protein coat that protects these genes, and some have an envelope of fat that surrounds them when they are outside a cell. (Viroids do not have a protein coat and prions contain no RNA or DNA.) Viruses vary from simple to very complex structures. Most viruses are about one hundred times smaller than an average bacterium. The origins of viruses in the evolutionary history of life are unclear: some may have evolved from plasmids—pieces of DNA that can move between cells—while others may have evolved from bacteria.

Viruses spread in many ways; plant viruses are often transmitted from plant to plant by insects that feed on sap, such as aphids, while animal viruses can be carried by blood-sucking insects. These disease-bearing organisms are known as vectors. Influenza viruses are spread by coughing and sneezing. HIV is one of several viruses transmitted through sexual contact and by exposure to infected blood. Viruses can infect only a limited range of host cells called the "host range." This can be broad, as a virus is capable of infecting many species or narrow. [4]

5. What can we infer from the first paragraph in this selection?

    a. A virus is the same as bacterium.

    b. A person with excellent vision can see a virus with the naked eye.

    c. A virus cannot be seen with the naked eye.

    d. Not all viruses are dangerous.

6. What types of organisms do viruses infect?

    a. Only plants and humans

    b. Only animals and humans

    c. Only disease-prone humans

    d. All types of organisms

7. How many parts do prions and viroids consist of?

    a. Two

    b. Three

    c. Either less than two or more than three

    d. Less than two

8. What is one common virus spread by coughing and sneezing?

    a. AIDS

    b. Influenza

    c. Herpes

    d. Tuberculosis

Questions 9 – 11 refer to the following passage.

Passage 3 – Thunderstorms

The first stage of a thunderstorm is the cumulus stage, or developing stage. In this stage, masses of moisture are lifted upwards into the atmosphere. The trigger for this lift can be insulation heating the ground producing thermals, areas where two winds converge, forcing air upwards, or, where winds blow over terrain of increasing elevation. Moisture in the air rapidly cools into liquid drops of water, which appears as cumulus clouds.

As the water vapor condenses into liquid, latent heat is released which warms the air, causing it to become less dense than the surrounding dry air. The warm air rises in an updraft through the process of convection (hence the term convective precipitation). This creates a low-pressure zone beneath the forming thunderstorm. In a typical thunderstorm, approximately 5×10^8 kg of water vapor is lifted, and the amount of energy released when this condenses is about equal to the energy used by a city of 100,000 in a month. [5]

9. The cumulus stage of a thunderstorm is the

    a. The last stage of the storm.

    b. The middle stage of the storm formation.

    c. The beginning of the thunderstorm.

    d. The period after the thunderstorm has ended.

10. One of the ways the air is warmed is

    a. Air moving downwards, which creates a high-pressure zone.

    b. Air cooling and becoming less dense, causing it to rise.

    c. Moisture moving downward toward the earth.

    d. Heat created by water vapor condensing into liquid.

11. Identify the correct sequence of events

    a. Warm air rises, water droplets condense, creating more heat, and the air rises further.

    b. Warm air rises and cools, water droplets condense, causing low pressure.

    c. Warm air rises and collects water vapor, the water vapor condenses as the air rises, which creates heat, and causes the air to rise further.

    d. None of the above.

Questions 12 – 15 refer to the following passage.

Passage 4 – US Weather Service

The United States National Weather Service classifies thunderstorms as severe when they reach a predetermined level. Usually, this means the storm is strong enough to inflict wind or hail damage. In most of the United States, a storm is considered severe if winds reach over 50 knots (58 mph or 93 km/h), hail is ¾ inch (2 cm) diameter or larger, or if meteorologists report funnel clouds or tornadoes. In the Central Region of the United States National Weather Service, the hail threshold for a severe thunderstorm is 1 inch (2.5 cm) in diameter. Though a funnel cloud or tornado shows the presence of a severe thunderstorm, the various meteorological agencies would issue a tornado warning rather than a severe thunderstorm warning.

Meteorologists in Canada define a severe thunderstorm as either having tornadoes, wind gusts of 90 km/h or greater, hail 2 centimeters in diameter or greater, rainfall more than 50 millimeters in 1 hour, or 75 millimeters in 3 hours.

Severe thunderstorms can develop from any type of thunderstorm. [6]

12. What is the purpose of this passage?

    a. Explaining when a thunderstorm turns into a tornado.

    b. Explaining who issues storm warnings, and when these warnings should be issued.

    c. Explaining when meteorologists consider a thunderstorm severe.

    d. None of the above.

13. It is possible to infer from this passage that

    a. Different areas and countries have different criteria for determining a severe storm.

    b. Thunderstorms can include lightning and tornadoes, as well as violent winds and large hail.

    c. If someone spots both a thunderstorm and a tornado, meteorological agencies will immediately issue a severe storm warning.

    d. Canada has a different alert system for severe storms, with criteria that are far less.

14. What would the Central Region of the United States National Weather Service do if hail was 2.7 cm in diameter?

    a. Not issue a severe thunderstorm warning.

    b. Issue a tornado warning.

    c. Issue a severe thunderstorm warning.

    d. Sleet must also accompany the hail before the Weather Service will issue a storm warning.

15. When would a tornado warning be issued instead of a thunderstorm warning.

    a. A tornado warning would be issued when there is a funnel cloud or a tornado.

    b. A tornado warning would be issued when there is a funnel cloud.

    c. A tornado warning is issued when there is a severe thunderstorm.

    d. None of the above.

Questions 16 – 19 refer to the following passage.

Passage 5 - If You Have Allergies, You're Not Alone

People who experience allergies might joke that their immune systems have let them down or are seriously lacking. Truthfully though, people who experience allergic reactions or allergy symptoms during certain times of the year have heightened immune systems that are, "better" than those of people who have perfectly healthy but less militant immune systems.

Still, when a person has an allergic reaction, they are having an adverse reaction to a substance that is considered normal to most people. Mild allergic reactions usually have symptoms like itching, runny nose, red eyes, or bumps or discoloration of the skin. More serious allergic reactions, such as those to animal and insect poisons or certain foods, may result in the closing of the throat, swelling of the eyes, low blood pressure, inability to breathe, and can even be fatal.

Different treatments help different allergies, and which one a person uses depends on the nature and severity of the allergy. It is recommended to patients with severe allergies to take extra precautions, such as carrying an EpiPen, which treats anaphylactic shock and may prevent death, always in order for the remedy to be readily available and more effective. When an allergy is not so severe, treatments may be used just relieve a person of uncomfortable symptoms. Over the counter allergy medicines treat milder symptoms, and can be bought at any grocery store and used in moderation to help people with allergies live normally.

There are many tests available to assess whether a person has allergies or what they may be allergic to, and advances in these tests and the medicine used to treat patients continues to improve. Despite this fact, allergies still affect many people throughout the year or even every day. Medicines used to treat allergies have side effects of their own, and it is difficult to bring the body into balance with the use of medicine. Regardless, many of those who live with allergies are grateful for what is available and find it useful in maintaining their lifestyles.

Practice Test Questions 1

16. According to this passage, it can be understood that the word "militant" belongs in a group with the words:

    a. sickly, ailing, faint

    b. strength, power, vigor

    c. active, fighting, warring

    d. worn, tired, breaking down

17. The author says that "medicines used to treat allergies have side effects of their own" to

    a. point out that doctors aren't very good at diagnosing and treating allergies.

    b. argue that because of the large number of people with allergies, a cure will never be found.

    c. explain that allergy medicines aren't cures and some compromise must be made.

    d. argue that more wholesome remedies should be researched and medicines banned.

18. It can be inferred that _____ recommend that some people with allergies carry medicine with them.

    a. the author

    b. doctors

    c. the makers of EpiPen

    d. people with allergies

19. The author has written this passage to

    a. inform readers on symptoms of allergies so people with allergies can get help.

    b. persuade readers to be proud of having allergies.

    c. inform readers on different remedies so people with allergies receive the right help.

    d. describe different types of allergies, their symptoms, and their remedies.

Questions 20 – 23 refer to the following passage.

Passage 6 – Clouds

A cloud is a visible mass of droplets or frozen crystals floating in the atmosphere above the surface of the Earth or other planetary bodies. Another type of cloud is a mass of material in space, attracted by gravity, called interstellar clouds and nebulae. The branch of meteorology which studies clouds is called nephrology. When we are speaking of Earth clouds, water vapor is usually the condensing substance, which forms small droplets or ice crystal. These crystals are typically 0.01 mm in diameter. Dense, deep clouds reflect most light, so they appear white, at least from the top. Cloud droplets scatter light very efficiently, so the farther into a cloud light travels, the weaker it gets. This accounts for the gray or dark appearance at the base of large clouds. Thin clouds may appear to have acquired the color of their environment or background. [7]

20. What are clouds made of?

    a. Water droplets

    b. Ice crystals

    c. Ice crystals and water droplets

    d. Clouds on Earth are made of ice crystals and water droplets

21. The main idea of this passage is

    a. Condensation occurs in clouds, having an intense effect on the weather on the surface of the earth.

    b. Atmospheric gases are responsible for the gray color of clouds just before a severe storm happens.

    c. A cloud is a visible mass of droplets or frozen crystals floating in the atmosphere above the surface of the Earth or other planetary body.

    d. Clouds reflect light in varying amounts and degrees, depending on the size and concentration of the water droplets.

Practice Test Questions 1   55

22. The branch of meteorology that studies clouds is called

    a. Convection

    b. Thermal meteorology

    c. Nephology

    d. Nephelometry

23. Why are clouds white on top and grey on the bottom?

a. Because water droplets inside the cloud do not reflect light, it appears white, and the farther into the cloud the light travels, the less light is reflected making the bottom appear dark.

b. Because water droplets outside the cloud reflect light, it appears dark, and the farther into the cloud the light travels, the more light is reflected making the bottom appear white.

c. Because water droplets inside the cloud reflects light, making it appear white, and the farther into the cloud the light travels, the more light is reflected making the bottom appear dark.

d. None of the above.

Questions 24 - 27 refer to the following recipe.

Passage 7 - When a Poet Longs to Mourn, He Writes an Elegy

Poems are an expressive, especially emotional, form of writing. They have been present in literature virtually from the time civilizations invented the written word. Poets often portrayed as moody, secluded, and even troubled, but this is because poets are introspective and feel deeply about the current events and cultural norms they are surrounded with. Poets often produce the most telling literature, giving insight into the society and mind set they come from. This can be done in many forms.

The oldest types of poems often include many stanzas, may or may not rhyme, and are more about telling a story than experimenting with language or words. The most common types of ancient poetry are epics, which are usually extremely long stories that follow a hero through his journey, or ellegies, which are often solemn in tone and used to mourn or lament something or someone. The Mesopotamians are often said to have invented the written word, and their literature is among the oldest in the world, including the epic poem titled "Epic of Gilgamesh." Similar in style and length to "Gilgamesh" is "Beowulf," an ellegy poem written in Old English and set in Scandinavia. These poems are often used by professors as the earliest examples of literature.

The importance of poetry was revived in the Renaissance. At this time, Europeans discovered the style and beauty of ancient Greek arts, and poetry was among those. Shakespeare is the most well-known poet of the time, and he used poetry not only to write poems but also to write plays for the theater. The most popular forms of poetry during the Renaissance included villanelles, sonnets, as well as the epic. Poets during this time focused on style and form, and developed very specific rules and outlines for how an exceptional poem should be written.

As often happens in the arts, modern poets have rejected the constricting rules of Renaissance poets, and free form poems are much more popular. Some modern poems would read just like stories if they weren't arranged into lines and stanzas. It is difficult to tell which poems and poets will be the most important, because works of art often become more famous in hindsight, after the poet has died and society can look at itself without being in the moment. Modern poetry continues to develop, and will continue to change as values, thought, and writing continue to change.

Poems can be among the most enlightening and uplifting texts for a person to read if they are looking to connect with the past, connect with other people, or try to gain an understanding of what is happening in their time.

24. In summary, the author has written this passage

    a. as a foreword that will introduce a poem in a book or magazine.

    b. because she loves poetry and wants more people to like it.

    c. to give a brief history of poems.

    d. to convince students to write poems.

25. The author organizes the paragraphs mainly by

    a. moving chronologically, explaining which types of poetry were common in that time.

    b. talking about new types of poems each paragraph and explaining them a little.

    c. focusing on one poet or group of people and the poems they wrote.

    d. explaining older types of poetry so she can talk about modern poetry.

26. The author's claim that poetry has been around "virtually from the time civilizations invented the written word" is supported by the detail that

a. Beowulf is written in Old English, which is not really in use any longer.

b. epic poems told stories about heroes.

c. the Renaissance poets tried to copy Greek poets.

d. the Mesopotamians are credited with both inventing the word and writing "Epic of Gilgamesh."

27. According to the passage, it can be understood that the word "telling" means

a. speaking

b. significant

c. soothing

d. wordy

Questions 28 – 32 refer to the following passage.

Passage 8 – Navy Seals

The United States Navy's Sea, Air and Land Teams, commonly known as Navy SEALs, are the U.S. Navy's principle special operations force, and a part of the Naval Special Warfare Command (NSWC) as well as the maritime component of the United States Special Operations Command (USSOCOM).

The unit's acronym ("SEAL") comes from their capacity to operate at sea, in the air, and on land – but it is their ability to work underwater that separates SEALs from most other military units in the world. Navy SEALs are trained and have been deployed in a wide variety of missions, including direct action and special reconnaissance operations, unconventional warfare, foreign internal defence, hostage rescue, counter-terrorism and other missions. All SEALs are members of either the United States Navy or the United States Coast Guard.

In the early morning of May 2, 2011 local time, a team of 40 CIA-led Navy SEALs completed an operation to kill Osama bin Laden in Abbottabad, Pakistan about 35 miles (56 km) from Islamabad, the country's capital. The Navy SEALs were part of the Naval Special Warfare Development Group, previously called "Team 6." President Barack Obama later confirmed the death of bin Laden. The unprecedented media coverage raised the public profile of the SEAL community, particularly the counter-terrorism specialists commonly known as SEAL Team 6. [8]

28. Are Navy SEALs part of USSOCOM?

a. Yes
b. No
c. Only for special operations
d. No, they are part of the US Navy

29. What separates Navy SEALs from other military units?

a. Belonging to NSWC
b. Direct action and special reconnaissance operations
c. Working underwater
d. Working for other military units in the world

30. What other military organizations do SEALs belong?

a. The US Navy
b. The Coast Guard
c. The US Army
d. The Navy and the Coast Guard

31. What other organization participated in the Bin Laden raid?

a. The CIA
b. The US Military
c. Counter-terrorism specialists
d. None of the above

32. What is the new name for Team 6?

a. They were always called Team 6
b. The counter-terrorism specialists
c. The Naval Special Warfare Development Group
d. None of the above

Practice Test Questions 1   *59*

Questions 33 – 36 refer to the following passage.

Passage 9 - Winged Victory of Samothrace: the Statue of the Gods

Students who read about the "Winged Victory of Samothrace" probably won't be able to picture what this statue looks like. However, almost anyone who knows about statues will recognize it when they see it: it is the statue of a winged woman who does not have arms or a head. Even the most famous pieces of art may be recognized by sight but not by name.

This iconic statue is of the Greek goddess Nike, who represented victory and was called Victoria by the Romans. The statue is sometimes called the "Nike of Samothrace." She was often displayed in Greek art as driving a chariot, and her speed or efficiency with the chariot may be what her wings symbolize. It is said that the statue was created around 200 BC to celebrate a battle that was won at sea. Archaeologists and art historians believe the statue may have originally been part of a temple or other building, even one of the most important temples, Megaloi Theoi, just as many statues were used during that time.

"Winged Victory" does indeed appear to have had arms and a head when it was originally created, and it is unclear why they were removed or lost. Indeed, they have never been discovered, even with all the excavation that has taken place. Many speculate that one of her arms was raised and put to her mouth, as though she was shouting or calling out, which is consistent with the idea of her as a war figure. If the missing pieces were ever to be found, they might give Greek and art historians more of an idea of what Nike represented or how the statue was used.

Learning about pieces of art through details like these can help students remember time frames or locations, as well as learn about the people who occupied them.

33. The author's title says the statue is "of the Gods" because

a. the statue is very beautiful and even a god would find it beautiful.

b. the statue is of a Greek goddess, and gods were of primary importance to the Greek.

c. Nike lead the gods into war.

d. the statues were used at the temple of the gods and so it belonged to them.

34. The third paragraph states that

a. the statue is related to war and was probably broken apart by foreign soldiers.

b. the arms and head of the statue cannot be found because all the excavation has taken place.

c. speculations have been made about what the entire statue looked like and what it symbolized.

d. the statue has no arms or head because the sculptor lost them.

35. The author's main purpose in writing this passage is to

a. demonstrate that art and culture are related and one can teach us about the other.

b. persuade readers to become archeologists and find the missing pieces of the statue.

c. teach readers about the Greek goddess Nike.

d. to teach readers the name of a statue they probably recognize.

36. The author specifies the indirect audience as "students" because

a. it is probably a student who is taking this test.

b. most young people don't know much about art yet and most young people are students.

c. students read more than people who are not students.

d. the passage is based on a discussion of what we can learn about culture from art.

Questions 37 – 40 refer to the following passage.

Passage 10 - Gardens

Ancient Roman gardens are known for their statues and sculptures, which were never missing from the lives of Romans. Romans designed their gardens with hedges and vines as well as a wide variety of flowers, including acanthus, cornflowers and crocus, cyclamen, hyacinth, iris and ivy, lavender, lilies, myrtle, narcissus, poppy, rosemary and violet. Flower beds were popular in the courtyards of the rich Romans.

The Middle Ages was a period of decline in gardening. After the fall of Rome, gardening was only to grow medicinal herbs and decorating church altars.

Islamic gardens were built after the model of Persian gardens, with enclosed walls and watercourses dividing the garden into four. Commonly, the center of the garden would have a pool or pavilion. Mosaics and glazed tiles used to decorate elaborate fountains are specific to Islamic gardens. [8]

37. What is a characteristic feature of Roman gardens?

    a. Statues and sculptures

    b. Flower beds

    c. Medicinal herbs

    d. Courtyard gardens

38. When did gardening decline?

    a. Before the Fall of Rome

    b. Gardening did not decline

    c. Before the Middle Ages

    d. After the Fall of Rome

39. What kind of gardening was done during the Middle Ages?

    a. Gardening with hedges and vines

    b. Gardening with a wide variety of flowers

    c. Gardening for herbs and church alters

    d. Gardening divided by watercourses

40. What is a characteristic feature of Islamic Gardens?

    a. Statues and Sculptures

    b. Decorative tiles and fountains

    c. Herbs

    d. Flower beds

Section III
Part II – Vocabulary

41. Choose a verb that means fearless or invulnerable to intimidation and fear.

    a. Feeble

    b. Strongest

    c. Dauntless

    d. Super

42. Choose a word that means the same as the underlined word.

I see the differences when they are placed side-by-side and <u>juxtaposed.</u>

    a. Compared

    b. Eliminated

    c. Overturned

    d. Exonerated

43. Choose the best definition of regicide.

    a. v. To endow or furnish with requisite ability, character, knowledge and skill

    b. n. killing of a king

    c. adj. Disposed to seize by violence or by unlawful or greedy methods

    d. v. To refresh after labor

44. Choose the best definition of pernicious.

    a. Deadly

    b. Infectious

    c. Common

    d. Rare

45. Fill in the blank.

After she received her influenza vaccination, Nan thought that she was _____ to the common cold.

- a. Immune
- b. Susceptible
- c. Vulnerable
- d. At risk

46. Choose a word that means the same as the underlined word.

She performed the gymnastics and stretches so well! I have never seen anyone so <u>nimble</u>.

- a. Awkward
- b. Agile
- c. Quick
- d. Taut

47. Choose a word that means the same as the underlined word.

Are there any more <u>queries</u>? We have already had so many questions today.

- a. Questions
- b. Commands
- c. Obfuscations
- d. Paradoxes

48. Choose a verb that means to remove a leader or high official from position.

- a. Sack
- b. Suspend
- c. Depose
- d. Dropped

49. Choose the best definition of pedestrian.

    a. Rare

    b. Often

    c. Walking or Running

    d. Commonplace

50. Choose the best definition of petulant.

    a. Patient

    b. Childish

    c. Impatient

    d. Mature

51. Fill in the blank.

Paul's rose bushes were being destroyed by Japanese beetles, so he invested in a good _____.

    a. Fungicide

    b. Fertilizer

    c. Sprinkler

    d. Pesticide

52. Choose the best definition of salient.

    a. v. To make light by fermentation, as dough

    b. adj. Not stringent or energetic

    c. adj. negligible

    d. adj. worthy of note or relevant

53. Choose the best definition of sedentary.

    a. n. A morbid condition, due to obstructed excretion of bile or characterized by yellowing of the skin

    b. adj. not moving or sitting in one place

    c. v. To wander from place to place

    d. n. Perplexity

54. Fill in the blank.

The last time that the crops failed, the entire nation experienced months of _____.

    a. Famine

    b. Harvest

    c. Plenitude

    d. Disease

55. Choose the best definition of stint.

    a. Thrifty

    b. Annoyed

    c. Dislike

    d. Insult

56. Choose the best definition of precipitate.

    a. To rain

    b. To throw down

    c. To throw up

    d. to snow

57. Choose the verb that means to build up or strengthen in relation to morals or religion.

    a. Sanctify

    b. Amplify

    c. Edify

    d. Wry

58. Choose the noun that means exit or way out.

    a. Door-jamb

    b. Egress

    c. Regress

    d. Furtherance

59. Choose the best definition of the underlined word.

The tide was in this morning but now it is starting to <u>recede</u>.

    a. Go out

    b. Flow

    c. Swell

    d. Come in

60. Choose the word that means private, personal.

    a. Confidential

    b. Hysteric

    c. Simplistic

    d. Promissory

Section IV – Math

1. A square lawn has an area of 62,500 square meters. What is the cost of building fence around it at a rate of $5.5 per meter?

    a. $4000

    b. $4500

    c. $5000

    d. $5500

2. The following numbers are the ages of people on a bus – 3, 6, 27, 13, 6, 8, 12, 20, 5, 10. Calculate their average of their ages.

    a. 11

    b. 6

    c. 9

    d. 110

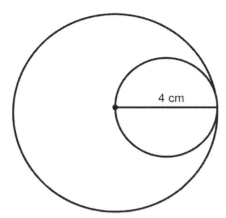

Note: Figure not drawn to scale

3. What is (area of large circle) - (area of small circle) in the figure above? Assume the diameter of the small circle is the radius of the larger circle.

    a. 8 π cm²

    b. 10 π cm²

    c. 12 π cm²

    d. 16 π cm²

4. Estimate 4,210,987 – 210,078

    a. 4,000,000

    b. 40,000,000

    c. 400,000

    d. 40,000

5. A distributor purchased 550 kilograms of potatoes for $165. He distributed these at a rate of $6.4 per 20 kilograms to 15 shops, $3.4 per 10 kilograms to 12 shops and the remainder at $1.8 per 5 kilograms. If his total distribution cost is $10, what will his profit be?

    a. $10.4

    b. $13.6

    c. $14.9

    d. $23.4

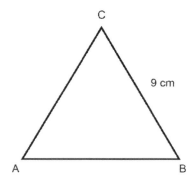

Note: figure not drawn to scale

6. What is the perimeter of the equilateral △ABC above?

    a. 18 cm
    b. 12 cm
    c. 27 cm
    d. 15 cm

7. How much pay does Mr. Johnson receive if he gives half of his pay to his family, $250 to his landlord, and has exactly 3/7 of his pay left after these expenses?

    a. $3600
    b. $3500
    c. $2800
    d. $1750

8. A boy has 4 red, 5 green and 2 yellow balls. He chooses two balls randomly. What is the probability that one is red and other is green?

    a. 2/11
    b. 19/22
    c. 20/121
    d. 9/11

9. Smith and Simon are playing a card game. Smith will win if a card drawn from a deck of 52 is either a 7 or a diamond, and Simon will win if the drawn card is an even number. Which statement is more likely to be correct?

    a. Simon will win more games.

    b. Smith will win more games.

    c. They have same winning probability.

    d. A decision cannot be made from the provided data.

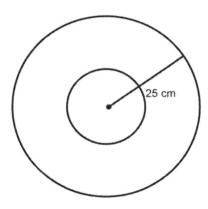

Note: Figure not drawn to scale

10. What is the distance travelled by the wheel above, when it makes 175 revolutions?

    a. 87.5 π m

    b. 875 π m

    c. 8.75 π m

    d. 8750 π m

11. How much water can be stored in a cylindrical container 5 meters in diameter and 12 meters high?

    a. 235.65 m³
    b. 223.65 m³
    c. 240.65 m³
    d. 252.65 m³

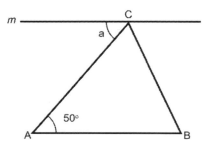

Note: Figure not drawn to scale

12. If the line m is parallel to the side AB of △ABC, what is angle a?

    a. 130°
    b. 25°
    c. 65°
    d. 50°

13. Estimate 215 x 65.

    a. 1,350
    b. 13,500
    c. 103,500
    d. 3,500

14. 4/5 – 2/3

    a. 2/2
    b. 2/13
    c. 1
    d. 2/15

15. If the speed of a train is 72 kilometers per hour, what distance will it

cover in 12 seconds?

    a. 200 m
    b. 220 m
    c. 240 m
    d. 260 m

16. In a class of 83 students, 72 are present. What percent of the students are absent? Provide answer up to two significant digits.

    a. 12%
    b. 13%
    c. 14%
    d. 15%

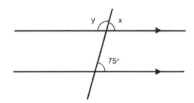

17. What is the value of the angle y?

    a. 25°
    b. 15°
    c. 30°
    d. 105°

18. A driver traveled from city A to city B in 1 hour and 13 minutes. On the way, he had to stop at 5 traffic signals, with an average time of 80 seconds. If the distance between the cities is 65 kilometers then what was the average driving speed?

    a. 56.42
    b. 58.77
    c. 60.34
    d. 63.25

19. A small business owner deposits $6000 in a savings account at a local bank. After 2 years, at 3% interest rate, what will be the interest earned?

    a. $6360

    b. $360

    c. $240

    d. $460

20. Richard gives 's' amount of salary to each of his 'n' employees weekly. If he has 'x' amount of money then how many days he can employ these 'n' employees.

    a. sx/7n

    b. 7x

    c. nx/7x

    d. 7x/ns

21. Mr. Micheal runs a factory. His total assets are $256,800 that consists of a building worth $80,500, machinery worth $125.000 and $51,300 cash. After one year what will be the value of his total assets if he has additional cash of $75,600 and the value of his building has increased by 10% per year, and his machinery depreciated by 20% per year?

    a. $243,450

    b. $252,450

    c. $264,150

    d. $272,350

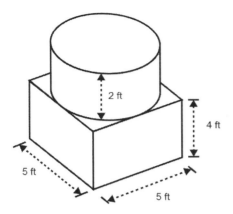

Note: Figure not drawn to scale

22. What is the approximate total volume of the above solid?

    a. 120 ft³
    b. 100 ft³
    c. 140 ft³
    d. 160 ft³

23. Martin earns $25,000 as basic pay, $500 rent and $860 for medical insurance. He spends 40% of his total earning on food and clothing, 10% on children's education and pays $800 for utility bills. What percent of his earning he is saving?

    a. 54%
    b. 50%
    c. 47%
    d. 44%

24. Below is the attendance for a class of 45.

Day	Absent Students
Monday	5
Tuesday	9
Wednesday	4
Thursday	10
Friday	6

What is the average attendance for the week?

    a. 88%

    b. 85%

    c. 81%

    d. 77%

25. Prize money of $1,050 is to be shared among top three contestants in ratio of 7:5:3 as 1st, 2nd and 3rd prizes respectively. How much more money will the 1st prize contestant receive than the 3rd prize contestant?

    a. $210

    b. $280

    c. $350

    d. $490

26. The manager of a weaving factory estimates that if 10 machines run on 100% efficiency for 8 hours, they will produce 1450 meters of cloth. Due to some technical problems, 4 machines run of 95% efficiency and the remaining 6 at 90% efficiency. How many meters of cloth can these machines will produce in 8 hours?

    a. 1334 meters

    b. 1310 meters

    c. 1300 meters

    d. 1285 meters

27. A driver at a speed of 's' miles per hour can reach his destination in 'h' hours. If his speed increased from 's' to 'x' then how much less time in hours will it take to reach his destination?

    a. $h - xh/s$

    b. $h - sh/x$

    c. s/x

    d. sh/x

28. A car covers a distance in 3.5 hours at an average speed of 60 km/hr. How much time in hours will a motorbike take to cover this distance at an average speed of 40km/hr?

    a. 4.5

b. 4.75

c. 5

d. 5.25

29. A grandfather is 8 times older than his grandson is now. After 6 years, he will be 5 times older than his grandson will. How old is the grandfather now?

a. 48

b. 56

c. 64

d. 72

30. Solve for n. 5n + (19 – 2)) = 67.

a. 21

b. 10

c. 15

d. 7

31. A boy is given 2 apples while his sister is given 8 oranges. What is the ratio between the boy's apples and her oranges?

a. 1:2

b. 2:4

c. 1:4

d. 2:1

32. Solve for x. 5x + 21 = 66.

a. 19

b. 9

c. 15

d. 5

33. What is the least common multiple of 9 and 3?

a. 27

b. 9

c. 3

d. 18

34. A box contains 7 black pencils and 28 blue ones. What is the ratio between the black and blue pens?

a. 1:4

b. 2:7

c. 1:8

d. 1:9

Practice Test Questions 1

35. If X + (32 + 356) = 920. What is x?

    a. 450

    b. 388

    c. 532

    d. 623

36. A boy buys 10 candies. The packet contains 3 green candies, 12 red and 9 blue candies. What is the ratio the green, red and blue sweets?

    a. 1:3:4

    b. 1:4:3

    c. 2:3:1

    d. 1:5:4

37. Solve for x. (12 x 12)/x = 12

    a. 12

    b. 13

    c. 8

    d. 14

38. Solve for A. A – (34 x 2) = 18.

    a. 86

    b. 78

    c. 50

    d. 73

39. Solve for X. X% of 120 = 30.

    a. 15

    b. 12

    c. 4

    d. 25

40. Solve for X. X * 25% of 100 = 75.

    a. 5

    b. 3

    c. 21

    d. 13

41. There are 12 people sitting in a bus and 3 people standing. What is the ratio between the people sitting and standing?

    a. 4:2

    b. 3:1

    c. 1:4

    d. 4:1

42. Solve for X. X% of 250 = 50.

    a. 30

    b. 35

    c. 25

    d. 20

43. Write 41.061 to the nearest 10th.

    a. 41.1

    b. 41.06

    c. 41

    d. 41.6

44. What is the least common multiple of 4 and 3?

    a. 24

    b. 6

    c. 16

    d. 12

45. Write 51.738 to the nearest 100th.

    a. 51.735

    b. 51.7

    c. 51.73

    d. 51.74

46. What is the ratio between 2 gold coins, 6 silver coins and 12 bronze coins?

    a. 2:3:4

    b. 1:2:4

    c. 1:3:4

    d. 2:3:4

47. What is the least common multiple of 8 and 12?

    a. 24

    b. 36

    c. 12

    d. 8

48. Solve for x. -7 + 3x = 20.

    a. 7

    b. 5

    c. 4

    d. 9

49. What is the least common multiple of 2 and 3?

    a. 2

    b. 4

    c. 6

    d. 3

Practice Test Questions 1

50. Solve for a, when 23 = 2a + 13.

    a. 6
    b. 12
    c. 5
    d. 8

51. Write 301.311 to the nearest 100th.

    a. 301.3
    b. 301.31
    c. 301
    d. 301.311

52. What is the least common multiple of 5 and 3?

    a. 35
    b. 25
    c. 15
    d. 12

53. Solve for c, when 124 = 12c - 20.

    a. 6
    b. 12
    c. 10
    d. 15

54. Write 765.3682 to the nearest 1000th.

    a. 765.368
    b. 765.361
    c. 765.369
    d. 765.378

55. Simplify 3 8/9 + 5 5/6.

    a. 8 13/15

    b. 8 3/9

    c. 9 13/18

    d. 8 12/18

56. Write 731.614 to the nearest 10th.

    a. 731.6

    b. 731.61

    c. 731.62

    d. 73

57. Simplify 7 4/5 + 2 2/5.

    a. 5 3/5

    b. 5 1/5

    c. 4 2/5

    d. 5 2/5

58. Write 765.3682 to the nearest 1000th.

    a. 765.368

    b. 765.361

    c. 765.369

    d. 765.378

59. Translate the following into an equation: three plus a number times 7 equals 42.

    a. $7(3 + X) = 42$

    b. $3(X + 7) = 42$

    c. $3X + 7 = 42$

    d. $(3 + 7)X = 42$

60. Estimate 5205 / 25

    a. 108

    b. 308

    c. 208

    d. 408

Section V – Language Arts

1. Choose the sentence below with the correct punctuation.

    a. Marcus who won the debate tournament, is the best speaker that I know.

    b. Marcus, who won the debate tournament, is the best speaker that I know.

    c. Marcus who won the debate tournament is the best speaker that I know.

    d. Marcus who won the debate tournament is the best speaker, that I know.

2. Choose the sentence below with the correct punctuation.

    a. To make chicken soup you must first buy a chicken.

    b. To make chicken soup you must first, buy a chicken.

    c. To make chicken soup, you must first buy a chicken.

    d. To make chicken soup; you must first buy a chicken.

3. Choose the sentence below with the correct punctuation.

    a. To travel around the globe you have to drive 25,000 miles.

    b. To travel around the globe, you have to drive 25000 miles.

    c. To travel around the globe, you have to drive, 25000 miles.

    d. To travel around the globe, you have to drive 25,000 miles.

4. Choose the sentence below with the correct punctuation.

a. The dog loved chasing bones, but never ate them; it was running that he enjoyed.

b. The dog loved chasing bones; but never ate them, it was running that he enjoyed.

c. The dog loved chasing bones, but never ate them, it was running that he enjoyed.

d. The dog loved chasing bones; but never ate them: it was running that he enjoyed.

5. Choose the sentence below with the correct punctuation.

a. He had not paid the rent, therefore, the landlord changed the locks.

b. He had not paid the rent; therefore, the landlord changed the locks.

c. He had not paid the rent, therefore; the landlord changed the locks.

d. He had not paid the rent therefore, the landlord changed the locks.

6. Choose the sentence below with the correct punctuation.

a. Jessica's father was in the Navy, so she attended schools in Newark, New Jersey, Key   West, Florida, San Diego, California, and Fairbanks, Alaska.

b. Jessica's father was in the Navy, so she attended schools in: Newark, New Jersey, Key West, Florida, San Diego, California, and Fairbanks, Alaska.

c. Jessica's father was in the Navy, so she attended schools in Newark, New Jersey; Key West, Florida; San Diego, California; and Fairbanks, Alaska.

d. Jessica's father was in the Navy, so she attended schools in Newark; New Jersey, Key West; Florida, San Diego, California, and Fairbanks, Alaska.

7. Choose the sentence below with the correct punctuation.

a. George wrecked John's car that was the end of their friendship.

b. George wrecked John's car. that was the end of their friendship.

c. George wrecked John's car; that was the end of their friendship.

d. None of the above

8. Choose the sentence below with the correct punctuation.

a. The dress was not Gina's favorite; however, she wore it to the dance.

b. The dress was not Gina's favorite, however, she wore it to the dance.

c. The dress was not Gina's favorite, however; she wore it to the dance.

d. The dress was not Gina's favorite however, she wore it to the dance.

9. Choose the sentence below with the correct punctuation.

a. Chris showed his dedication to golf in many ways, for example, he watched all of the tournaments on television.

b. Chris showed his dedication to golf in many ways; for example, he watched all of the   tournaments on television.

c. Chris showed his dedication to golf in many ways, for example; he watched all of the tournaments on television.

d. Chris showed his dedication to golf in many ways for example he watched all of the tournaments on television.

10. Choose the sentence with the correct capitalization.

a. I was able to speak with Susan Roberts, Mayor of Tampa.

b. I was able to speak with Susan Roberts, mayor of Tampa.

c. I was able to speak with Susan Roberts, Mayor of tampa.

d. None of the Above.

11. Choose the sentence with the correct capitalization.

a. I think thanksgiving is the best fall holiday.

b. I think Thanksgiving is the best Fall holiday.

c. I think Thanksgiving is the best fall holiday.

d. None of the above.

12. Choose the sentence with the correct capitalization.

a. I will be skipping the Fall 2012 Semester.

b. I will be skipping the fall 2012 semester.

c. I will be skipping the Fall 2012 semester.

d. None of the above.

13. Choose the sentence with the correct capitalization.

a. They speak Spanish in Mexico.

b. They speak spanish in Mexico.

c. They speak spanish in mexico.

d. None of the above.

14. Choose the sentence with the correct capitalization.

a. My best friend said, "always count your change."

b. My best friend said, "Always Count your Change."

c. My best friend said, "Always count your change."

d. None of the above.

15. Choose the sentence with the correct capitalization.

a. The Victorian Era was in the nineteenth century.

b. The victorian era was in the nineteenth century.

c. The Victorian Era was in the Nineteenth century.

d. The Victorian era was in the Nineteenth century.

16. Choose the sentence with the correct capitalization.

a. I prefer Pepsi to coke.

b. I prefer pepsi to Coke.

c. I prefer Pepsi to Coke.

d. None of the above.

17. Choose the sentence with the correct capitalization.

a. I always have french fries with my coke.

b. I always have french fries with my Coke.

c. I always have French Fries with my Coke.

d. None of the above.

18. Choose the sentence with the correct capitalization.

a. The blue jays are my favorite team.

b. the blue Jays are my favorite team.

c. The Blue Jays are my favorite team.

d. The blue Jays are my favorite team.

19. Choose the sentence with the correct capitalization.

a. The Southwest is the best part of the country.

b. The southwest is the best part of the country.

c. The southwest is the best part of the Country.

d. None of the above.

20. Choose the sentence with the correct capitalization.

a. My favorite Dylan song is blowin' in the wind.

b. My favorite dylan song is Blowin' in the Wind.

c. My favorite Dylan song is Blowin' in the Wind.

d. None of the above.

21. Choose the sentence with the correct capitalization.

a. My latest novel, Danger on the Rhine will be published next year.

b. My latest novel, danger on the Rhine will be published next year.

c. My latest novel, danger on the rhine will be published next year.

d. None of the above.

22. Choose the sentence with the correct usage.

a. The Chinese live in one of the world's most populous nations, while a citizen of Bermuda lives in one of the least populous.

b. The Chinese lives in one of the world's most populous nations, while a citizen of Bermuda live in one of the least populous.

c. The Chinese live in one of the world's most populous nations, while a citizen of Bermuda live in one of the least populous.

d. The Chinese lives in one of the world's most populous nations, while a citizen of Bermuda lives in one of the least populous.

23. Choose the sentence with the correct usage.

a. Disease is highly prevalent in poorer nations; the most dominant disease is malaria.

b. Disease are highly prevalent in poorer nations; the most dominant disease is malaria.

c. Disease is highly prevalent in poorer nations; the most dominant disease are malaria.

d. Disease are highly prevalent in poorer nations; the most dominant disease are malaria.

24. Choose the sentence with the correct usage.

a. Although I would prefer to have dog, I actually own a cat.

b. Although I would prefer to have a dog, I actually own cat.

c. Although I would prefer to have a dog, I actually own a cat.

d. Although I would prefer to have dog, I actually own cat.

25. Choose the sentence with the correct usage.

a. The principal of the school lived by one principle: always do your best.

b. The principle of the school lived by one principle: always do your best.

c. The principal of the school lived by one principal: always do your best.

d. The principle of the school lived by one principal: always do your best.

26. Choose the sentence with the correct usage.

a. Even with an speed limit sign clearly posted, an inattentive driver may drive too fast.

b. Even with a speed limit sign clearly posted, a inattentive driver may drive too fast.

c. Even with an speed limit sign clearly posted, a inattentive driver may drive too fast.

d. Even with a speed limit sign clearly posted, an inattentive driver may drive too fast.

27. Choose the sentence with the correct usage.

a. Except for the roses, she did not accept John's frequent gifts.

b. Accept for the roses, she did not except John's frequent gifts.

c. Accept for the roses, she did not accept John's frequent gifts.

d. Except for the roses, she did not except John's frequent gifts.

28. Choose the sentence with the correct usage.

a. Although he continued to advise me, I no longer took his advice.

b. Although he continued to advice me, I no longer took his advise.

c. Although he continued to advise me, I no longer took his advise.

d. Although he continued to advice me, I no longer took his advise.

29. Choose the sentence with the correct usage.

a. To adopt to the climate, we had to adopt a different style of clothing.

b. To adapt to the climate, we had to adapt a different style of clothing.

c. To adapt to the climate, we had to adopt a different style of clothing.

d. None of the above are correct.

30. Choose the sentence with the correct usage.

a. When he's between friends, Robert seems confident, but, between you and me, he is very shy.

b. When he's among friends, Robert seems confident, but, among you and me, he is very shy.

c. When he's between friends, Robert seems confident, but, among you and me, he is very shy.

d. When he's among friends, Robert seems confident, but, between you and me, he is very shy.

31. Choose the sentence with the correct usage.

a. I will be finished at ten in the morning, and will be arriving at home at about 6:30.

b. I will be finished at about ten in the morning, and will be arriving at home at 6:30.

c. I will be finished at about ten in the morning, and will be arriving at home at about 6:30.

d. I will be finished at ten in the morning, and will be arriving at home at 6:30.

32. Choose the sentence with the correct usage.

a. Beside the red curtains and pillows, there was a red rug beside the couch.

b. Besides the red curtains and pillows, there was a red rug beside the couch.

c. Besides the red curtains and pillows, there was a red rug besides the couch.

d. Beside the red curtains and pillows, there was a red rug besides the couch.

33. Choose the sentence with the correct usage.

a. Although John can swim very well, the lifeguard may not allow him to swim in the pool.

b. Although John may swim very well, the lifeguard may not allow him to swim in the pool.

c. Although John can swim very well, the lifeguard can not allow him to swim in the pool.

d. None of the choices are correct.

34. Choose the sentence with the correct usage.

a. Her continuous absences caused a continual disruption at the office.

b. Her continual absences caused a continuous disruption at the office.

c. Her continual absences caused a continual disruption at the office.

d. Her continuous absences caused a continuous disruption at the office.

Practice Test Questions 1   91

35. Choose the sentence with the correct usage.

a. During the famine, the Irish people had to emigrate to other countries; many of them immigrated to the United States.

b. During the famine, the Irish people had to immigrate to other countries; many of them immigrated to the United States.

c. During the famine, the Irish people had to emigrate to other countries; many of them emigrated to the United States.

d. During the famine, the Irish people had to immigrate to other countries; many of them emigrated to the United States.

36. Choose the sentence with the correct usage.

a. His home was farther than we expected; farther, the roads were very bad.

b. His home was farther than we expected; further, the roads were very bad.

c. His home was further than we expected; further, the roads were very bad.

d. His home was further than we expected; farther, the roads were very bad.

37. Choose the sentence with the correct usage.

a. The volunteers brought groceries and toys to the homeless shelter; the latter were given to the staff, while the former were given directly to the children.

b. The volunteers brought groceries and toys to the homeless shelter; the former was given to the staff, while the latter was given directly to the children.

c. The volunteers brought groceries and toys to the homeless shelter; the groceries were given to the staff, while the former was given directly to the children.

d. The volunteers brought groceries and toys to the homeless shelter; the latter was given to the staff, while the groceries were given directly to the children.

38. Choose the sentence with the correct grammar.

a. His doctor suggested that he eat less snacks and do fewer lounging on the couch.

b. His doctor suggested that he eat fewer snacks and do less lounging on the couch.

c. His doctor suggested that he eat less snacks and do less lounging on the couch.

d. His doctor suggested that he eat fewer snacks and do fewer lounging on the couch.

39. Choose the sentence with the correct grammar.

    a. However, I believe that he didn't really try that hard.

    b. However I believe that he didn't really try that hard.

    c. However; I believe that he didn't really try that hard.

    d. However: I believe that he didn't really try that hard.

40. Choose the sentence with the correct grammar.

    a. There was however, very little difference between the two.

    b. There was, however very little difference between the two.

    c. There was; however, very little difference between the two.

    d. There was, however, very little difference between the two.

41. Choose the sentence with the correct grammar.

    a. Don would never have thought of that book, but you could have reminded him.

    b. Don would never of thought of that book, but you could have reminded him.

    c. Don would never have thought of that book, but you could of have reminded him.

    d. Don would never of thought of that book, but you could of reminded him.

42. Choose the sentence with the correct grammar.

    a. The mother would not of punished her daughter if she could have avoided it.

    b. The mother would not have punished her daughter if she could of avoided it.

    c. The mother would not of punished her daughter if she could of avoided it.

    d. The mother would not have punished her daughter if she could have avoided it.

43. Choose the sentence with the correct grammar.

a. There was scarcely no food in the pantry, because nobody ate at home.

b. There was scarcely any food in the pantry, because nobody ate at home.

c. There was scarcely any food in the pantry, because not nobody ate at home.

d. There was scarcely no food in the pantry, because not nobody ate at home.

44. Choose the sentence with the correct grammar.

a. Although you may not see nobody in the dark, it does not mean that nobody is there.

b. Although you may not see anyone in the dark, it does not mean that not nobody is there.

c. Although you may not see anyone in the dark, it does not mean that anyone is there.

d. Although you may not see nobody in the dark, it does not mean that not nobody is there.

45. Choose the sentence with the correct grammar.

a. Michael has lived in that house for forty years, while I has owned this one for only six weeks.

b. Michael have lived in that house for forty years, while I have owned this one for only six weeks.

c. Michael have lived in that house for forty years, while I has owned this one for only six weeks.

d. Michael has lived in that house for forty years, while I have owned this one for only six weeks.

46. Choose the sentence with the correct grammar.

a. The older children have already eat their dinner, but the baby has not yet eaten anything.

b. The older children have already eaten their dinner, but the baby has not yet ate anything.

c. The older children have already eaten their dinner, but the baby has not yet eaten anything.

d. The older children have already eat their dinner, but the baby has not yet ate anything.

47. Choose the sentence with the correct grammar.

    a. If they had gone to the party, he would have gone too.

    b. If they had went to the party, he would have gone too.

    c. If they had gone to the party, he would have went too.

    d. If they had went to the party, he would have went too.

48. Choose the sentence with the correct grammar.

    a. He should have went to the appointment; instead, he went to the beach.

    b. He should have gone to the appointment; instead, he went to the beach.

    c. He should have went to the appointment; instead, he gone to the beach.

    d. He should have gone to the appointment; instead, he gone to the beach.

49. Choose the correct spelling.

    a. humoros

    b. humouros

    c. humorous

    d. humorus

50. Choose the correct spelling.

    a. knowlege

    b. knowledge

    c. knowlegde

    d. knowlledge

51. Choose the correct spelling.

    a. camaraderie

    b. camaredere

    c. camaradere

    d. cameraderie

52. Choose the correct spelling.

a. mathematics

b. mathmatics

c. matematics

d. mathamatics

53. Choose the correct spelling.

a. conscentious

b. conscientios

c. conscientious

d. consceintious

54. Choose the correct spelling.

a. leisuire

b. lesure

c. lesure

d. leisure

55. Choose the correct spelling.

a. pigeone

b. pigoen

c. pigeon

d. pidgeon

56. Choose the correct spelling.

a. odyessy

b. odeyssey

c. odysey

d. odyssey

57. Choose the correct spelling.

    a. sacreligious

    b. sacriligious

    c. sacrilegious

    d. sacrilegous

58. Choose the correct spelling.

    a. accommodate

    b. accomodate

    c. acommodate

    d. accommodaite

59. Choose the correct spelling.

    a. consenssus

    b. conssensus

    c. consensus

    d. consemsus

60. Choose the correct spelling.

    a. exhilirate

    b. exhalirate

    c. exhilerate

    d. exhilarate

Answer Key

Section 1 – Verbal Skills

1. C

This is a functional relationship. A lawyer defends a client in a trial in the same way a doctor performs an operation on a patient.

2. B

This is a cause and effect relationship. You must eat to become fat, in the same way you must breathe to live.

3. D

This is a definition relationship. A dog is a canine in the same way a porpoise is a mammal.

4. A

This is a time relationship. A turntable is an early type of stereo, MP3 player is a modern stereo. In the same way, a horse drawn carriage is an earlier type of car.

5. B

This is a type relationship. A cub is a young bear, in the same way a puppy is a young dog.

6. A

Law cures anarchy in the same way medicine cures illness.

7. B

This is a type relationship. Gold is a type of metal in the same way a surgeon is a type of doctor.

8. C

This is a process relationship. The first word is the process which creates the second. For example, ice melts to liquid in the same way water freezes to create a solid.

9. D

This is a measurement relationship. Clocks measure time in the same way thermometers measure temperature.

10. C

A car is kept in a garage the same way a plane is kept in a hangar.

11. B

Peculiar and strange are synonyms.

12. B
Tippet and shawl are synonyms.

13. D
Vivid and brilliant are synonyms.

14. B
Semblance and image are synonyms.

15. A
Impregnable and unconquerable are synonyms.

16. A
Jargon and slang are synonyms.

17. A
Render and give are synonyms.

18. B
Intrusive and invasive are synonyms.

19. A
Renowned and popular are synonyms.

20. C
Incoherent and jumbled are synonyms.

21. A
Congenial and pleasant are synonyms.

22. D
Plight and situation are synonyms.

23. A
Berate and criticize are synonyms.

24. B
Sate and satisfy are synonyms.

25. B
Terminate and end are synonyms.

26. C
This is a repetition pattern. All the choices repeat a 3 number sequence.

27. D
This is a word meaning relationship. Pain is not a synonym for any of the choic-

es.

28. D

This is a repetition vowel pattern. All the choices have 3 vowels except D.

29. D

This is a vowel and consonant relationship. All the choices have a vowel at the end, except abc.

30. C

This is a repetition pattern. All the choices repeat a 2-letter sequence obtained by adding 2 to the previous number.

31. B

This is a word meaning relationship. Lean is not a synonym for any of the choices.

32. B

This is a capital small letter relationship. All choices have alternate letters capitalized.

33. D

This is a relationship of words question. All the choices are synonyms of look and see, except surmise.

34. D

This is a word meaning relationship. List is not a synonym for any of the choices.

35. A

This is a word meaning relationship. List is not a synonym for any of the choices.

36. C

This is a capital letter small letter relationship. All the choices begin with a capital letter, as well as beginning with a consonant.

37. D

This is a relationship of words question. All the choices are dog or canine family except cougar.

38. C

This is a word meaning relationship. Overweight is not a synonym for any of the choices.

39. A

This is a relationship of words question. All the choices are synonyms of great, except smart.

40. D
This is a word meaning relationship. Command is not a synonym for any of the choices.

41. A
This is a word meaning relationship. Assume is not a synonym for any of the choices.

42. C
Discord and harmony are antonyms.

43. B
Latter and former are antonyms.

44. C
Shrink and expand are antonyms.

45. B
Reluctant and enthusiastic are antonyms.

46. D
Refute and agree are antonyms.

47. C
Vulnerable and strong are antonyms.

48. D
Intrepid and timid are antonyms.

49. A
Liaise and uncoordinated are antonyms.

50. D
Ridicule and praise are antonyms.

51. B
Fixed and indefinite are antonyms.

52. A
The antonym of flamboyant is plain.

53. C
The antonym of sporadic is regular.

54. Uncertain.
It does not say where they went swimming.

Practice Test Questions 1

55. True
It must be true that if fish use their gills to breathe, and fish can't breathe out of water, then gills don't work out of water.
56. Uncertain.
It does not say that they eat steak every time they are hungry.

57. Uncertain.
It does not say where they went swimming. There could be Herman Melville books they can't find or haven't read.

58. True
The answer because the first statement says 'all.' Therefore the conclusion is also true. If the first sentence did NOT say 'all,' the conclusion would not be true.

59. True
The conclusion must be true, since all cats are mammals. The conclusion would be false if the first statement was 'all,' and the second statement was 'some.'

60. False
Although all students carry a backpack, not everyone who carries a backpack is a student. I.e. there are some people who carry a backpack who are not students.

Section II – Quantitative Skills

1. A
The interval begins with 5, increases by 2 and is added each time.

2. C
The numbers in Box B are squares of the numbers in Box A, so the missing number in Box B is 9.

3. B
The numbers in Box B are result of (number in Box A * 2) + 3. Therefore, the missing number is 21.

4. A
The number doubles each time.

5. D
The numbers decrease by 6 each time.

6. C
Each number is the sum of the previous two numbers.

7. D
The number triples each time.

8. A
The number in row B is 4 times the number in row A.
9. C
Each number is ten less than the next number. E.g. 29 is 10 less than 39.

10. B
One letter is missing after each letter.

11. A
Two letters are missing after each letter.

12. D
Each number is 7 greater than the previous.

13. A
The sequence increases initially and then decreases in the next term. The relationship between each increase is +3 and the relationship with the alternate decrease is -3. So the answer is -2 from the last given term. $13 - 2 = 11$.

14. B
The sequence is decreasing by half. So half of $1/4 = 1/8$

15. D
This sequence is increasing by adding 6.

16. B
The sequence is increasing by adding an increasing amount to the previous number e.g. 4, 5, 6, 7, 8, 9....etc. The next term is of the sequence is $26 + 7 = 33$ and then $33 + 8 = 41$

17. B
The second term decreased by 3, and the subsequent terms decreased at twice the last rate of decrease. The next term of the sequence is thus $-4 - 24 = -28$. The 6th term is $-28 - 48 = -76$.

18. A
The sequence is increasing by 4.

19. B
20. B
21. D
22. B
23. C
24. A
25. C
26. C

27. A

28. B
#1 = 16
#2 = 33
#3 = 22
1 < 2 > 3

29. B
1. 96
2. 44
3. 84
4. 9
1 > 4 < 3

30. C
#1 = 23
#2 = 31
#3 = 28
#4 = 22
2 > 1 < 3

31. A
#1 = 32
#2 = 3
#3 = 12
#4 = 22
2 is the smallest.

32. D
#1 = 43
#2 = 15
#3 = 35
#4 = 42
None of the Above.

33. A
#1 = 39
#2 = 3
#3 = 28
1 > 2 < 3

34. D
1. 25
2. 32
3. 15
4. 20
(#1 + #2) = 57 > 20

35. D

#1 = 216
#2 = 38
#3 = 36
None of the Above.

36. C
a. 4% of 4 = .16
b. 5% of 5 = 0.25
c. 0.3% of 12 = 0.036
d. 1/5 of 100 = 20
C is the smallest.

37. C
2/5 of 20 = 8 + 8 = 16

38. A
50% of 50 = 25 + 6 = 31

39. B
3/4 of 40 = 30 + 7 = 37
100 − X = 37
X = 63

40. A
x/5 = 1/4 * 100
x/5 = 25
x = 125

41. C
1/5X = 5 * 10
1/5X = 50
x = 250

42. A
5z = 52 − 10
Z = 10.4 − 2
Z = 8.4

43. D
25 - Z = 1/5 X 20
25 - Z = 4
Z = 21

44. C
Z = (3/5 * 40) - 15
Z = 24 - 15
Z = 9

45. B
Z = 10 X (1/2 X 60)
Z = 10 X 30
Z = 300

46. C
8 X 10 = 80
1/4Z = 80
Z = 4 X 80
Z = 320

47. A
4 X 15 = 60
1/2 x = 60
X = 120

48. B
5 X 60 = 300
300 = 1/3X
x = 900

49. D
4 X 8 = 32
1/4 X + 20 = 32
1/4 X = 12
x = 48

50. B
3/4 or 100 = 75
500 - x = 75 + 10
500 - x = 85
x = 500 - 85
x = 415

Section III – Reading

1. B
We can infer from this passage that sickness from an infectious disease can be easily transmitted from one person to another.

From the passage, "Infectious pathologies are also called communicable diseases or transmissible diseases, due to their potential of transmission from one person or species to another by a replicating agent (as opposed to a toxin)."

2. A
Two other names for infectious pathologies are communicable diseases and trans-

missible diseases.

From the passage, "Infectious pathologies are also called communicable diseases or transmissible diseases, due to their potential of transmission from one person or species to another by a replicating agent (as opposed to a toxin)."

3. C
Infectivity describes the ability of an organism to enter, survive and multiply in the host. This is taken directly from the passage, and is a definition type question.

Definition type questions can be answered quickly and easily by scanning the passage for the word you are asked to define.

"Infectivity" is an unusual word, so it is quick and easy to scan the passage looking for this word.

4. B
We know an infection is not synonymous with an infectious disease because an infection may not cause important clinical symptoms or impair host function.

5. C
We can infer from the passage that, a virus is too small to be seen with the naked eye. Clearly, if they are too small to be seen with a microscope, then they are too small to be seen with the naked eye.

6. D
Viruses infect all types of organisms. This is taken directly from the passage, "Viruses infect all types of organisms, from animals and plants to bacteria and single-celled organisms."

7. C
The passage does not say exactly how many parts prions and viroids consist of. It does say, "**Unlike** prions and viroids, viruses consist of two or three parts ..." so prions and viroids are NOT like virus. We can therefore infer, they consist of either less than two or more than three parts.

8. B
A common virus spread by coughing and sneezing is Influenza.

9. C
The cumulus stage of a thunderstorm is the beginning of the thunderstorm.

This is taken directly from the passage, "The first stage of a thunderstorm is the cumulus, or developing stage."

10. D
The passage lists four ways that air is heated. One way is, heat created by water vapor condensing into liquid.

11. A

The sequence of events can be taken from these sentences:

As the moisture carried by the [1] air currents rises, it rapidly cools into liquid drops of water, which appear as cumulus clouds. As the water vapor condenses into liquid, it [2] releases heat, which warms the air. This in turn causes the air to become less dense than the surrounding dry air and [3] rise farther.

12. C

The purpose of this text is to explain when meteorologists consider a thunderstorm severe.

The main idea is the first sentence, "The United States National Weather Service classifies thunderstorms as severe when they reach a predetermined level." After the first sentence, the passage explains and elaborates on this idea. Everything is this passage is related to this idea, and there are no other major ideas in this passage that are central to the whole passage.

13. A

From this passage, we can infer that different areas and countries have different criteria for determining a severe storm.

From the passage we can see that most of the US has a criteria of, winds over 50 knots (58 mph or 93 km/h), and hail ¾ inch (2 cm). For the Central US, hail must be 1 inch (2.5 cm) in diameter. In Canada, winds must be 90 km/h or greater, hail 2 centimeters in diameter or greater, and rainfall more than 50 millimeters in 1 hour, or 75 millimeters in 3 hours.

Choice D is incorrect because the Canadian system is the same for hail, 2 centimeters in diameter.

14. C

With hail above the minimum size of 2.5 cm. diameter, the Central Region of the United States National Weather Service would issue a severe thunderstorm warning.

15. A

A tornado warning is issued where this is a funnel cloud or tornado, even though there may be a severe thunderstorm.

16. C

This question tests the reader's vocabulary skills. The uses of the negatives "but" and "less," especially right next to each other, may confuse readers into answering with choices A or D, which list words that are antonyms to "militant." Readers may also be confused by the comparison of healthy people with what is being described as an overly healthy person--both people are good, but the reader may look for which one is "worse" in the comparison, and therefore stray toward the antonym words. One key to understanding the meaning of "militant" if the reader is unfamiliar with it is to look at the root of the word; readers can then easily associate it with "military" and gain a sense of what the word signifies: defense (especially considered that the immune system defends the body). Choice C is correct over choice B because "militant" is an adjective, just as the words in choice C, whereas the words in choices B are nouns.

17. C

This question tests the reader's understanding of function within writing. The other choices are details included surrounding the quoted text, and may therefore confuse the reader. Choice A somewhat contradicts what is said earlier in the paragraph, which is, tests and treatments are improving, and probably doctors are along with them, but the paragraph doesn't actually mention doctors, and the subject of the question is the medicine. Choice B may seem correct to readers who aren't careful to understand that, while the author does mention the large number of people affected, the author is touching on the realities of living with allergies, rather than about the likelihood of curing all allergies. Similarly, while the author does mention the "balance" of the body, which is easily associated with "wholesome," the author is not really making an argument and especially is not making an extreme statement that allergy medicines should be outlawed. Again, because the article's tone is on living with allergies, choice C is an appropriate choice that fits with the title and content of the text.

18. B

This question tests the reader's inference skills. The text does not state who is doing the recommending, but the use of the "patients," as well as the general context of the passage, lends itself to the logical partner, "doctors," B. The author does mention the recommendation but doesn't present it as her own (i.e. "I recommend that"), so A may be eliminated. It may seem plausible that people with allergies (D) may recommend medicines or products to other people with allergies, but the text does not necessarily support this interaction taking place. C may be selected because the EpiPen is specifically mentioned, but the use of the phrase "such as" when it is introduced is not limiting enough to assume the recommendation is coming from its creators.

19. D

This question tests the reader's global understanding of the text. D includes the main topics of the three body paragraphs, and isn't too focused on a specific aspect or quote from the text, as the other questions are, giving a skewed summary of what the author intended. The reader may be drawn to B because of the title of the passage and the use of words like "better," but the message of the passage is larger and more general than this.

20. D

Clouds in space are made of different materials attracted by gravity. Clouds on Earth are made of water droplets or ice crystals.

Choice D is the best answer. Notice also that Choice D is the most specific.

21. C

The main idea is the first sentence of the passage; a cloud is a visible mass of droplets or frozen crystals floating in the atmosphere above the surface of the Earth or other planetary body.

The main idea is very often the first sentence of the paragraph.

22. C

Nephology, which is the study of cloud physics.

23. C

This question asks about the process, and gives choices that can be confirmed or eliminated easily.

From the passage, "Dense, deep clouds reflect most light, so they appear white, at least from the top. Cloud droplets scatter light very efficiently, so the farther into a cloud light travels, the weaker it gets. This accounts for the gray or dark appearance at the base of large clouds."

We can eliminate choice A, since water droplets inside the cloud do not reflect light is false.

We can eliminate choice B, since, water droplets outside the cloud reflect light, it appears dark, is false.

Choice C is correct.

24. C

This question tests the reader's summarization skills. The use of the word "actually" in describing what kind of people poets are, as well as other moments like this, may lead readers to selecting B or D, but the author is giving more information than trying to persuade readers. The author gives no indication that she loves poetry, (B) or that people, students specifically (D), should write poems. Choice A is incorrect because the style and content of this paragraph do not match those of a foreword; forewords usually focus on the history or ideas of a specific poem to introduce it more fully and help it stand out against other poems. The author here focuses on several poems and gives broad statements. Instead, she tells a kind of story about poems, giving three very broad time periods in which to discuss them, thereby giving a brief history of poetry, as answer C states.

25. A

This question tests the reader's summarization skills. Key words in the topic sentences of each of the paragraphs ("oldest," "Renaissance," "modern") should give the reader an idea that the author is moving chronologically. The opening and closing sentence-paragraphs are broad and talk generally. Choice B seems reasonable, but epic poems are mentioned in two paragraphs, eliminating the idea that only new types of poems are used in each paragraph. Choice C is also easily eliminated because the author clearly mentions several different poets, groups of people, and poems. D also seems reasonable, considering that the author does move from older forms of poetry to newer forms, but use of "so (that)" makes this statement false, for the author gives no indication that she is rushing (the paragraphs are about the same size) or that she prefers modern poetry.

26. D
This question tests the reader's attention to detail. The key word is "invented"-- it ties together the Mesopotamians, who invented the written word, and the fact that they, as the inventors, also invented and used poetry. The other selections focus on other details mentioned in the passage, such as that the Renaissance's admiration of the Greeks (C) and that Beowulf is in Old English (A). Choice B may seem like an attractive answer because it is unlike the others and because the idea of heroes seems rooted in ancient and early civilizations.

27. B
This question tests the reader's vocabulary and contextualization skills. "Telling" is not an unusual word, but it may be used here in a way that is not familiar to readers, as an adjective rather than a verb in gerund form. Choice A may seem like the obvious answer a reader looking for a verb to match the use they are familiar with. If the reader understands that the word is being used as an adjective and that choice A is a ploy, they may opt to select choice D, "wordy," but it does not make sense in context. Choice C can be easily eliminated, and doesn't have any connection to the paragraph or passage. "Significant" (B) does make sense contextually, especially relative to the phrase "give insight" used later in the sentence.

28. A
Navy SEALS are the maritime component of the United States Special Operations Command (USSOCOM).

29. C
Working underwater separates SEALs from other military units. This is taken directly from the passage.

30. D
SEALs also belong to the Navy and the Coast Guard.

31. A
The CIA also participated. From the passage, the raid was conducted by a "team of 40 *CIA-led* Navy SEALS."

32. C
From the passage, "The Navy SEALs were part of the Naval Special Warfare Development Group, previously called 'Team 6.' "

33. B
This question tests the reader's summarization skills. Choice A is a very broad

statement that may or may not be true, and seems to be in context, but has nothing to do with the passage. The author does mention that the statue was probably used on a temple dedicated to the Greek gods (D), but in no way discusses or argues for the gods' attitude toward, or claim on these temples or its faucets. Nike does indeed lead the gods into a war (the Titan war), as choice C suggests, but this is not mentioned by the passage and students who know this may be drawn to this answer but have not done a close enough analysis of the text that is actually in the passage. Choice B is appropriately expository, and connects the titular emphasis to the idea that the Greek gods are very important to Greek culture.

34. C
This question tests the reader's summarization skills. The text for choice C is pulled straight from the paragraph, but is not word for word, so it may seem too obvious to be the right answer. The passage does talk about Nike being the goddess of war, as choice A states, but the third paragraph only touches on it and it is an inference that soldiers destroyed the statue, when this question is asking specifically for what the third paragraph actually stated. Choice B is also straight from the text, with a minor but key change: the inclusion of the words "all" and "never" are too limiting and the passage does not suggest that these limits exist. If a reader selects choice D, they are also making an inference that is misguided for this type of question. The paragraph does state that the arms and head are "lost" but does not suggest who lost them.

35. A
This question tests the reader's ability to recognize function in writing. B can be eliminated based on the purpose of the passage, which is expository and not persuasive. The author may or may not feel this way, but the passage does not show evidence of being argumentative for that purpose. Choices C and D are both details found in the text, but, neither of them encompasses the entire message of the passage, which has an overall message of learning about culture from art and making guesses about how the two are related, as suggested by choice A.

36. D
This question tests the reader's ability to understand function within writing. Most of the possible selections are very general statements which may or may not be true. It probably is a student who is taking the test on which this question is featured (A), but the author makes no address to the test taker and is not talking to the audience in terms of the test. Likewise, it may also be true that students read more than adults (C), mandated by schools and grades, but the focus on the verb "read" in the first sentence is too narrow and misses the larger purpose of the passage; the same could be said for choice B. While all the statements could be true, choice D is the most germane, and infers the purpose of the passage without making assumptions that could be incorrect.

37. A
The ancient Roman gardens are known by their statues and sculptures ... from the first sentence.

38. D

After the fall of Rome, gardening was only for medicinal purposes, AND gardening declined in the Middle Ages, so we can infer gardening declined after the fall of Rome.

39. C

From the passage, "After the fall of Rome gardening was only done with the purpose of growing medicinal herbs and decorating church altars," so Choice C.

40. B

From the passage, "Mosaics and glazed tiles used to decorate elaborate fountains are specific to Islamic gardens."

41. C

Dauntless: adj. Invulnerable to fear or intimidation.

42. A

Juxtaposed: adj. Placed side by side often for comparison or contrast.

43. B

Regicide: v. killing of a king.

44. A

Pernicious: adj. Causing much harm in a subtle way.

45. A

Immune: adj. Resistant to a particular infection or toxin owing to the presence of specific antibodies.

46. B

Nimble: adj. Quick and light in movement or action.

47. A

Queries: n. Questions or inquiries.

48. C

Depose: To remove (a leader) from (high) office, without killing the incumbent.

49. D

Pedestrian: Ordinary, dull; everyday; unexceptional.

50. B

Petulant: adj. Childishly irritable.

51. D
Pesticide: n. A substance used for destroying insects or other organisms harmful to cultivated plants or to animals.

52. D
Salient: adj. worthy or note or relevant.

53. B
Sedentary: adj. not moving or sitting in one place.

54. A
Famine: n. extreme scarcity of food.

55. A
Stint: n. To be sparing, thrifty.

56. A
Precipitate: v. to rain.

57. C
Edify: v. To instruct or improve morally or intellectually.

58. B
Egress: n. An exit or way out.

59. A
Recede: v. To move back, to move away.

60. A
Confidential: adj. kept secret within a certain circle of persons; not intended to be known publicly.

Section IV – Mathematics

1. D
As the lawn is square, the length of one side will be the square root of the area. $\sqrt{62,500} = 250$ meters. So, the perimeter is found by 4 times the length of the side of the square:

$250 \cdot 4 = 1000$ meters.

Since each meter costs \$5.5, the total cost of the fence will be $1000 \cdot 5.5 = \$5,500$.

2. A

First add all the numbers $3 + 6 + 27 + 13 + 6 + 8 + 12 + 20 + 5 + 10 = 110$. Then divide by 10 (the number of data provided) $= 110/10 = 11$

3. C

In the figure, we are given a large circle and a small circle inside it; with the diameter equal to the radius of the large one. The diameter of the small circle is 4 cm. This means that its radius is 2 cm. Since the diameter of the small circle is the radius of the large circle, the radius of the large circle is 4 cm. The area of a circle is calculated by: пr2 where r is the radius.

Area of the small circle: $\pi(2)^2 = 4\pi$

Area of the large circle: $\pi(4)^2 = 16\pi$

The difference area is found by:

Area of the large circle - Area of the small circle $= 16\pi - 4\pi = 12\pi$

4. A

$4{,}210{,}987 - 210{,}078$ is about $4{,}000{,}000$.

5. B

The distribution is done in three different rates and amounts:

$6.4 per 20 kilograms to 15 shops ... $20 \cdot 15 = 300$ kilograms distributed

$3.4 per 10 kilograms to 12 shops ... $10 \cdot 12 = 120$ kilograms distributed

$550 - (300 + 120) = 550 - 420 = 130$ kilograms left. This amount is distributed by 5 kilogram portions. So, this means that there are $130/5 = 26$ shops.

$1.8 per 130 kilograms.

We need to find the amount he earned overall these distributions.

$6.4 per 20 kilograms : $6.4 \cdot 15 = 96 for 300 kilograms

$3.4 per 10 kilograms : $3.4 \cdot 12 = \$40.8$ for 120 kilograms

$1.8 per 5 kilograms : $1.8 \cdot 26 = \$46.8$ for 130 kilograms

So, he earned $96 + 40.8 + 46.8 = \$ 183.6$

The total distribution cost is given as $10

The profit is found by: Money earned - money spent ... It is important to remember that he bought 550 kilograms of potatoes for $165 at the beginning:

Profit $= 183.6 - 10 - 165 = \$8.6$

6. C
Equilateral triangle with 9 cm sides
Perimeter = 9+9+9
= 27 cm.

7. B
We check the fractions taking place in the question. We see that there is a "half" (that is 1/2) and 3/7. So, we multiply the denominators of these fractions to decide how to name the total money. We say that Mr. Johnson has 14x at the beginning; he gives half of this, meaning 7x, to his family. $250 to his landlord. He has 3/7 of his money left. 3/7 of 14x is equal to:

14x * (3/7) = 6x

So,

Spent money is: 7x + 250

Unspent money is: 6x

Total money is: 14x

We write an equation: total money = spent money + unspent money

14x = 7x + 250 + 6x

14x - 7x - 6x = 250

x = 250

We are asked to find the total money that is 14x:

14x = 14•250 = $3500

8. A
The probability that the 1st ball drawn is red = 4/11. The probability that the 2nd ball drawn is green = 5/10. The combined probability will then be 4/11 X 5/10 = 20/110 = 2/11.

9. B
There are 52 cards. Smith has 16 cards in which he can win. Therefore, his winning probability in a single game will be 16/52. Simon has 20 cards in which he can win, so his probability of winning in a single draw is 20/52.

10. A
The wheel travels 2пr distance when it makes one revolution. Here, r stands for the radius. The radius is given as 25 cm in the figure. So,

2пr = 2п * 25 = 50п cm is the distance travelled in one revolution.

Practice Test Questions 1

In 175 revolutions: 175•50п = 8750п cm is travelled.

We are asked to find the distance in meter.

1 m = 100 cm So;

8750п cm = 8750п / 100 = 87.5п m

11. B
The formula of the volume of cylinder is the base area multiplied by the height. As the formula:

Volume of a cylinder = пr2h. Where п is 3.142, r is radius of the cross sectional area, and h is the height.

We know that the diameter is 5 meters, so the radius is 5/2 = 2.5 meters.

The volume is: V = 3.142•2.52•12 = 235.65 m3.

12. D
Two parallel lines (m & side AB) intersected by side AC. This means that 50◦ and a angles are interior angles. So:
a = 50◦ (interior angles).

13. B
215 X 65 = 13975, or about 13,500.

14. D
A common denominator is needed, 12-10/15 = 2/15

15. C
1 hour is equal to 3600 seconds and 1 kilometer is equal to 1000 meters. Therefore, a train covers 72000 meters in 36000 seconds.

Distance covered in 12 seconds = 12 × 72000/3600 = 240 meters.

16. B
Number of absent students = 83 – 72 = 11

Percentage of absent students is found by proportioning the number of absent students to total number of students in the class = 11•100/83 = 13.25

Checking the answers, we round 13.25 to the nearest whole number: 13%

17. D
As shown in the figure, two parallel lines intersecting with a third line with angle of 75◦.

x = 75° (corresponding angles)

x + y = 180° (supplementary angles) … inserting the value of x here:

y = 180° - 75°
y = 105°

18. B
Time taken to travel from A to B in seconds = 3600 + (13 X 60) = 3600 + 780 = 4380 seconds.
Total time spent at traffic signals = 80 X 5 = 400 seconds.
The remaining driving time = 4380 – 400 = 3980 seconds = 3980/3600 = 1.106 hours
The speed will be 65/1.106 = 58.77 km/hr

19. B
I = ?, r = 3%, t = 2 years, P = 6000. Convert the rate to decimal. 3% = 0.03. Then plug in variables into the simple interest formula. I = P x r x t, I = 6000 x 0.03 x 2, I = $360

20. D
We understand that each of the n employees earn s amount of salary weekly. This means that one employee earns s salary weekly. So; Richard has ns amount of money to employ n employees for a week.

We are asked to find the number of days n employees can be employed with x amount of money. We can do simple direct proportion:

If Richard can employ n employees for 7 days with ns amount of money,

Richard can employ n employees for y days with x amount of money … y is the number of days we need to find.

We can do cross multiplication:

y = (x * 7)/(ns)

y = 7x/ns

21. C
Cash assets = 75600
Building assets after one year = 80500 X 1.1 = $88550
Machinery assets after one year = 125000 X 0.8 = 100,000
Total value of assets = 264150

22. C
Volume of a cylinder is π x r^2 x h
Diameter = 5 ft. so radius is 2.5 ft.

Volume of the cylinder = π x 2.5² x 2
= π x 6.25 x 2 = 12.5 π
Approximate π to 3.142
Volume of the cylinder = 39.25

Volume of a rectangle = height X width X length.
= 5 X 5 X 4 = 100

Total volume = Volume of rectangular solid + volume of cylinder
Total volume = 100 + 39.25
Total volume = 139.25 ft³ or approximately 140 ft³

23. C
Total earnings = 25000 + 500 + 860 = $26360
Food and Clothing expenses = 0.4 X 26360 = 10544
Children's education expense = 26360 X 0.1 = $2636
Utility Bills = $800
Savings = 26360 – 10544 – 2636 – 800 = $12380
Percent savings = 100 X 12380/26360 = 47%

24. B
Percentage attendance will be 85%

25. B
1st prize winner receives, 7 X 1050/15 = $490
3rd price winner receives, 3 X 1050/15 = $210
Difference = 490 – 210 = $280

26. A
At 100% efficiency 1 machine produces 1450/10 = 145 m of cloth.

At 95% efficiency, 4 machines produce 4•145•95/100 = 551 m of cloth.

At 90% efficiency, 6 machines produce 6•145•90/100 = 783 m of cloth.

Total cloth produced by all 10 machines = 551 + 783 = 1334 m

Since the information provided and the question are based on 8 hours, we did not
need to use time to reach the answer.

27. B
If the driver increases their speed from 's' to 'x' miles per hour, the equation will
be h - sh/x.

28. D
Distance covered by the car = 60 X 3.5 = 210 km.
Time required by the motorbike = 210/40 = 5.25 hr.

29. C
Let the grandson's age be X and the grandfather's age be Y. According we have,
y = 8x
and
y + 6 = 5(x + 6)
Solving we get y = 64

30. B
5n + (19 – 2)) = 67, 5n + 17 = 67, 5n = 67 -17, 5n = 50, n = 50/5 = 10

31. C
The ratio between apples and oranges is 2 to 8 or 2:8. Bring to the lowest terms by dividing both sides by 2 gives 1:4.

32. B
5x + 21 = 66, 5x = 66 – 21 = 45, 5x = 45, x = 45/5 = 9

33. B
Multiples of 3 are 3, 6, 9 and Multiples of 9 are 9, 18, therefore the least common multiple is 9.

34. A
The ratio between black and blue pens is 7 to 28 or 7:28. Bring to the lowest terms by dividing both sides by 7 gives 1:4.

35. C
32 + 356 = 388. Therefore X + 388 = 920, X = 920 – 388 = 532

36. B
The ratio between green, red and blue candies is 3:12:9. Bring to the lowest terms by dividing the sides by 3 gives 1:4:3.

37. A
12 x 12 = 144, so 144/x = 12
144 = 12X
X = 12

38. A
34 x 2 = 68, so A – 68 = 18, A = 68 + 18 = 86

39. D
X% of 120 = 30, so X = 30/120 x 100/1 = 300/12 = 25

40. B
X * (25% of 100) = 75,
25X = 75, X = 75/25 = 3
41. D

The ratio between people sitting and standing is 12 to 3 or 12:3. Bring to the lowest terms by dividing both sides by 3 gives 4:1.

42. D
X% of 250 = 50, so X = 50/250 x 100/1= 100/5 = 20

43. B
The number is 41.061. The last digit 1 is less than 5, and so it's discarded. The next digit, 6, is greater than 5 and so is removed and 1 is added to the next digit to the left. Answer = 41.1

44. D
Multiples of 3 are 3, 6, 9, 12 and Multiples of 4 are 4, 8, 12, Therefore the least common multiple is 12.

45. D
The number is 51.738. The last digit is greater than 5, so it is removed and 1 is added to the next number to the left. Answer = 51.74.

46. C
The ratio between gold, silver and bronze coins is 2:6:8. Bring to the lowest terms by dividing each side by 2 gives 1:3:4.

47. A
Multiples of 8 are 8, 16, 24 and multiples of 12 are 12, 24, 36, so the least common multiple is 24.

48. D
$3x = 20 + 7 = 27$, $x = 27/3$, $x = 9$.

49. C
Multiples of 2 are 2, 4, 6 and Multiples of 3 are 3, 6, so the least common is 6.

50. C
$23 = 2a + 13$, $23 - 13 = 2a$, $10 = 2a$, $a = 10/2 = 5$.

51. B
301.311, since the last digit is less than 5 it is removed. Answer = 301.31.

52. C
Multiples of 5 are 5, 10, 15, 20 and multiples of 3 are 3, 6, 9, 12, 15... so the answer is 15.

53. B
$124 = 12c - 20$, $124 + 20 = 12c$, $144 = 12c$, $c = 144/12 = 12$.

54. A

The number is 765.3682. The last digit, 2, is less than 5, so it is discarded. Answer = 765.368.

55. C
Add the whole numbers and then add the fractions, therefore 3 + 5 {8/9 + 5/6}, then find a common denominator for the fractions 8 {16/18 + 15/18} = 8 31/18, then simplify to 9 13/18

56. A
The number is 731.614. The last digit is less than 5 so it is removed. Answer = 731.6

57. D
Subtract the whole numbers and then subtract the fractions, therefore 7 - 2 {4/5 - 2/5}, the fractions has a common denominator, so
5 (4-2/5) = 5 2/5.

58. A
The number is 51.738. The last digit, 2, is less than 5, so it is discarded. Answer = 765.368.

59. C
Three plus a number times 7 equals 42. Let X be the number.
(3 + X) times 7 = 42
7(3 + X) = 42

60. C
5205 / 25 = 208.20 or, about 208.

Section V – Language Arts

1. B
Comma separate phrases.

2. C
The comma separates phrases.

3. D
To travel around the globe, you have to drive 25,000 miles.

4. A
The dog loved chasing bones, but never ate them; it was running that he enjoyed.

5. B
The semicolon links independent clauses with a conjunction (therefore).

6. C
Use a semicolon in a list where the list items have internal punctuation, such as "Key West, Florida."

7. C
The semicolon links independent clauses. An independent clause can form a complete sentence by itself.

8. A
The semicolon links independent clauses with a conjunction (However).

9. B
The semicolon links independent clauses. An independent clause can form a complete sentence by itself.

10. B
Titles preceding names are capitalized, but not titles that follow names.

11. C
Holidays are capitalized; the names of seasons are not.

12. C
The names of seasons are not capitalized because they are generic nouns. If a season is used in a title, such as the "Fall 2012 semester," Fall 2012 is a title and capitalized.

13. A
The names of languages and countries are capitalized.

14. C
Quoted speech is not capitalized.

15. A
Periods and events are capitalized but not century numbers.

16. C
Brand names are capitalized.

17. B
Brand names are capitalized by generic terms such as 'french fries' are not.

18. C
The names of sports teams, as proper nouns, are capitalized.

19. A
North, south, east, and west when used as sections of the country, are capitalized, but not as compass directions

20. C
The major words in the titles of books, articles, and songs are capitalized. (but not short prepositions or the articles "the," "a," or "an," if they are not the first word of the title)

21. A
Titles of publications are capitalized.

22. A
Singular subjects. "The Chinese" is plural, and "a citizen of Bermuda" is singular.

23. A
Disease is singular.

24. C
Articles of speech. Both dog and cat in this sentence are singular and require the article 'a.'

25. A
Principle vs. Principal. A principal is the First, highest, or foremost in importance, or rank. A principle is a fundamental truth.

26. D
A vs. An. The article 'a' come before a consonant and 'an' comes before a vowel.

27. A
Accept vs. Except. To accept is to receive or to say yes. Except is a preposition that means excluding.

28. A
Advise vs. Advice. To advise is to give advice. Advice is an opinion that someone offers.

29. C
Adapt vs. Adopt.
Adapt means "to change." Usually we adapt to someone or something. Adopt means "to take as one's own."

30. D
Among vs. Between. Among is for more than 2 items, and between is only for 2 items.

When he's among friends (many or more than 2), Robert seems confident, but,

Practice Test Questions 2

between you and I (two), he is very shy.

31. D
At vs. About. 'At' refers to a specific time and 'about' refers to a more general time. A common usage is 'at about 10,' but it isn't proper grammar.

32. B
Beside vs. Besides. 'Beside' means next to, and 'besides' means in addition to.

33. A
Can vs. May. 'Can' refers to ability and 'may' refers to permission.

Although John can swim (is able to. very well, he may not (permission. be allowed to swim in the pool.

34. B
Continual vs. Continuous. 'Continuous' means a time with no interruption and 'continual' means a time with interruption.

Her continual absences (with interruption – not always absent. caused a continuous disruption (the disruption was ongoing without interruption at the office.

35. A
Emigrate vs. Immigrate. 'To emigrate' means to leave one's country and to 'immigrate' means to come to a country.

36. B
Further vs. Farther. 'Farther' is used for physical distance, and 'further' is used for figurative distance.

37. B
Former vs. Latter. 'Former' refers to the first of two things, 'latter' to the second.

38. B
Fewer vs. Less. 'Fewer' is used with countables and 'less' is used with uncountables.

39. A
'However' usage. 'However' usually has a comma before and after.

40. D
'However' Usage. 'However' usually has a comma before and after.

41. A
The third conditional is used for talking about an unreal situation (that did not happen) in the past. For example, "If I had studied harder, [if clause] I would have passed the exam [main clause]. Which is the same as, "I failed the exam, because I didn't study hard enough."

42. D
The third conditional is used for talking about an unreal situation (that did not happen) in the past. For example, "If I had studied harder, [if clause] I would have passed the exam [main clause]. Which is the same as, "I failed the exam, because I didn't study hard enough."

43. B
Double negative sentence. In double negative sentences, one of the negatives is replaced with 'any.'

44. C
Double negative sentence. In double negative sentences, one of the negatives is replaced with 'any.'

45. D
Present perfect. You cannot use the present perfect with specific time expressions such as, yesterday, one year ago, last week, when I was a child, at that moment, that day, one day, etc. The Present Perfect is used with unspecific expressions such as, ever, never, once, many times, several times, before, so far, already, yet, etc.

46. C
Present perfect. You cannot use the Present Perfect with specific time expressions such as, yesterday, one year ago, last week, when I was a child, at that moment, that day, one day, etc. The Present Perfect is used with unspecific expressions such as, ever, never, once, many times, several times, before, so far, already, yet, etc.

47. A
Went vs. Gone. Went is the simple past tense. Gone is used in the past perfect.

48. B
Went vs. Gone. 'Went' is the simple past tense. 'Gone' is used in the past perfect.

49. C
50. B
51. A
52. A
53. C
54. D
55. C
56. D
57. C
58. A
59. C
60. D

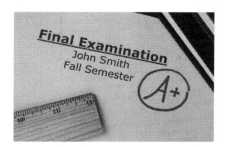

Practice Test Questions Set 2

THE QUESTIONS BELOW ARE NOT THE SAME AS YOU WILL FIND ON THE HSPT® - THAT WOULD BE TOO EASY! And nobody knows what the questions will be and they change all the time. Below are general questions that cover the same subject areas as the HSPT®. So, while the format and exact wording of the questions may differ slightly, and change from year to year, if you can answer the questions below, you will have no problem with the HSPT®.

For the best results, take these practice test questions as if it were the real exam. Set aside time when you will not be disturbed, and a location that is quiet and free of distractions. Read the instructions carefully, read each question carefully, and answer to the best of your ability.

Use the bubble answer sheets provided. When you have completed the practice questions, check your answer against the Answer Key and read the explanation provided.

Do not attempt more than one set of practice test questions in one day. After completing the first practice test, wait two or three days before attempting the second set of questions.

Section I – Verbal Skills
Questions: 60
Time: 16 Minutes

Section II – Quantitative Skills
Questions: 50
Time: 30 Minutes

Section III – Reading & Vocabulary
Questions: 62
Time: 25 Minutes

Section IV – Math
Questions: 60
Time: 45 Minutes

Section V – Language
Questions: 60
Time: 25 Minutes

Verbal Skills Answer Sheet

1. (A) (B) (C) (D)   21. (A) (B) (C) (D)   41. (A) (B) (C) (D)

2. (A) (B) (C) (D)   22. (A) (B) (C) (D)   42. (A) (B) (C) (D)

3. (A) (B) (C) (D)   23. (A) (B) (C) (D)   43. (A) (B) (C) (D)

4. (A) (B) (C) (D)   24. (A) (B) (C) (D)   44. (A) (B) (C) (D)

5. (A) (B) (C) (D)   25. (A) (B) (C) (D)   45. (A) (B) (C) (D)

6. (A) (B) (C) (D)   26. (A) (B) (C) (D)   46. (A) (B) (C) (D)

7. (A) (B) (C) (D)   27. (A) (B) (C) (D)   47. (A) (B) (C) (D)

8. (A) (B) (C) (D)   28. (A) (B) (C) (D)   48. (A) (B) (C) (D)

9. (A) (B) (C) (D)   29. (A) (B) (C) (D)   49. (A) (B) (C) (D)

10. (A) (B) (C) (D)   30. (A) (B) (C) (D)   50. (A) (B) (C) (D)

11. (A) (B) (C) (D)   31. (A) (B) (C) (D)   51. (A) (B) (C) (D)

12. (A) (B) (C) (D)   32. (A) (B) (C) (D)   52. (A) (B) (C) (D)

13. (A) (B) (C) (D)   33. (A) (B) (C) (D)   53. (A) (B) (C) (D)

14. (A) (B) (C) (D)   34. (A) (B) (C) (D)   54. (A) (B) (C) (D)

15. (A) (B) (C) (D)   35. (A) (B) (C) (D)   55. (A) (B) (C) (D)

16. (A) (B) (C) (D)   36. (A) (B) (C) (D)   56. (A) (B) (C) (D)

17. (A) (B) (C) (D)   37. (A) (B) (C) (D)   57. (A) (B) (C) (D)

18. (A) (B) (C) (D)   38. (A) (B) (C) (D)   58. (A) (B) (C) (D)

19. (A) (B) (C) (D)   39. (A) (B) (C) (D)   59. (A) (B) (C) (D)

20. (A) (B) (C) (D)   40. (A) (B) (C) (D)   60. (A) (B) (C) (D)

Quantitative Skills Answer Sheet

1. A B C D
2. A B C D
3. A B C D
4. A B C D
5. A B C D
6. A B C D
7. A B C D
8. A B C D
9. A B C D
10. A B C D
11. A B C D
12. A B C D
13. A B C D
14. A B C D
15. A B C D
16. A B C D
17. A B C D

18. A B C D
19. A B C D
20. A B C D
21. A B C D
22. A B C D
23. A B C D
24. A B C D
25. A B C D
26. A B C D
27. A B C D
28. A B C D
29. A B C D
30. A B C D
31. A B C D
32. A B C D
33. A B C D
34. A B C D

35. A B C D
36. A B C D
37. A B C D
38. A B C D
39. A B C D
40. A B C D
41. A B C D
42. A B C D
43. A B C D
44. A B C D
45. A B C D
46. A B C D
47. A B C D
48. A B C D
49. A B C D
50. A B C D

Reading Comprehension and Vocabulary Answer Sheet

1. A B C D
2. A B C D
3. A B C D
4. A B C D
5. A B C D
6. A B C D
7. A B C D
8. A B C D
9. A B C D
10. A B C D
11. A B C D
12. A B C D
13. A B C D
14. A B C D
15. A B C D
16. A B C D
17. A B C D
18. A B C D
19. A B C D
20. A B C D

21. A B C D
22. A B C D
23. A B C D
24. A B C D
25. A B C D
26. A B C D
27. A B C D
28. A B C D
29. A B C D
30. A B C D
31. A B C D
32. A B C D
33. A B C D
34. A B C D
35. A B C D
36. A B C D
37. A B C D
38. A B C D
39. A B C D
40. A B C D

41. A B C D
42. A B C D
43. A B C D
44. A B C D
45. A B C D
46. A B C D
47. A B C D
48. A B C D
49. A B C D
50. A B C D
51. A B C D
52. A B C D
53. A B C D
54. A B C D
55. A B C D
56. A B C D
57. A B C D
58. A B C D
59. A B C D
60. A B C D

Mathematics Answer Sheet

1. (A) (B) (C) (D)
2. (A) (B) (C) (D)
3. (A) (B) (C) (D)
4. (A) (B) (C) (D)
5. (A) (B) (C) (D)
6. (A) (B) (C) (D)
7. (A) (B) (C) (D)
8. (A) (B) (C) (D)
9. (A) (B) (C) (D)
10. (A) (B) (C) (D)
11. (A) (B) (C) (D)
12. (A) (B) (C) (D)
13. (A) (B) (C) (D)
14. (A) (B) (C) (D)
15. (A) (B) (C) (D)
16. (A) (B) (C) (D)
17. (A) (B) (C) (D)
18. (A) (B) (C) (D)
19. (A) (B) (C) (D)
20. (A) (B) (C) (D)

21. (A) (B) (C) (D)
22. (A) (B) (C) (D)
23. (A) (B) (C) (D)
24. (A) (B) (C) (D)
25. (A) (B) (C) (D)
26. (A) (B) (C) (D)
27. (A) (B) (C) (D)
28. (A) (B) (C) (D)
29. (A) (B) (C) (D)
30. (A) (B) (C) (D)
31. (A) (B) (C) (D)
32. (A) (B) (C) (D)
33. (A) (B) (C) (D)
34. (A) (B) (C) (D)
35. (A) (B) (C) (D)
36. (A) (B) (C) (D)
37. (A) (B) (C) (D)
38. (A) (B) (C) (D)
39. (A) (B) (C) (D)
40. (A) (B) (C) (D)

41. (A) (B) (C) (D)
42. (A) (B) (C) (D)
43. (A) (B) (C) (D)
44. (A) (B) (C) (D)
45. (A) (B) (C) (D)
46. (A) (B) (C) (D)
47. (A) (B) (C) (D)
48. (A) (B) (C) (D)
49. (A) (B) (C) (D)
50. (A) (B) (C) (D)
51. (A) (B) (C) (D)
52. (A) (B) (C) (D)
53. (A) (B) (C) (D)
54. (A) (B) (C) (D)
55. (A) (B) (C) (D)
56. (A) (B) (C) (D)
57. (A) (B) (C) (D)
58. (A) (B) (C) (D)
59. (A) (B) (C) (D)
60. (A) (B) (C) (D)

Language Arts Answer Sheet

1. A B C D
2. A B C D
3. A B C D
4. A B C D
5. A B C D
6. A B C D
7. A B C D
8. A B C D
9. A B C D
10. A B C D
11. A B C D
12. A B C D
13. A B C D
14. A B C D
15. A B C D
16. A B C D
17. A B C D
18. A B C D
19. A B C D
20. A B C D

21. A B C D
22. A B C D
23. A B C D
24. A B C D
25. A B C D
26. A B C D
27. A B C D
28. A B C D
29. A B C D
30. A B C D
31. A B C D
32. A B C D
33. A B C D
34. A B C D
35. A B C D
36. A B C D
37. A B C D
38. A B C D
39. A B C D
40. A B C D

41. A B C D
42. A B C D
43. A B C D
44. A B C D
45. A B C D
46. A B C D
47. A B C D
48. A B C D
49. A B C D
50. A B C D
51. A B C D
52. A B C D
53. A B C D
54. A B C D
55. A B C D
56. A B C D
57. A B C D
58. A B C D
59. A B C D
60. A B C D

Section I – Verbal Skills

Choose the word with the same relationship as the given pair.

1. **Acting : Theater :: Gambling :** _____

    a. Gym

    b. Bar

    c. Club

    d. Casino

2. **Pork : Pig :: Beef :** _____

    a. Herd

    b. Farmer

    c. Cow

    d. Lamb

3. **Fruit : Banana :: Mammal :** _____

    a. Rabbit

    b. Snake

    c. Fish

    d. Sparrow

4. **Slumber : Sleep :: Bog :** _____

    a. Dream

    b. Foray

    c. Swamp

    d. Night

5. **Petal: Flower :: Fur :** _____

    a. Coat

    b. Warm

    c. Woman

    d. Rabbit

6. Present : Birthday :: Reward : _____

    a. Accomplishment

    b. Medal

    c. Acceptance

    d. Cash

7. Shovel : Dig :: Scissors : _____

    a. Scoop

    b. Carry

    c. Snip

    d. Rip

8. Finger : Hand :: Leg : _____

    a. Body

    b. Foot

    c. Toe

    d. Hip

Choose the pair with the same relationship

9. Zoology : Animals

    a. Ecology : Pollution

    b. Botany : Plants

    c. Chemistry : Atoms

    d. History : People

10. Child : Human

    a. Dog : Pet

    b. Kitten : Cat

    c. Cow : Milk

    d. Bird : Robin

11. Wax : Candle

    a. Ink : Pen

    b. Clay : Bowl

    c. String : Kite

    d. Liquid : Cup

12. Choose the synonym pair.

    a. Pensive and Alibi

    b. Able and Competent

    c. Allow and Forbid

    d. Capable and Honest

13. Choose the synonym pair.

    a. Antidote and Cure

    b. Potion and Lure

    c. Craft and Magic

    d. Affiliation and Member

14. Choose the synonym pair.

    a. Quality and Measure

    b. Compensation and Wage

    c. Consensus and Agreement

    d. Command and Obey

15. Choose the synonym pair.

    a. Magnify and Amplify

    b. Emphasize and Trace

    c. Blot and Shade

    d. Stamina and Agility

16. Choose the synonym pair.

    a. Haphazard and Order

    b. Immaculate and Perfect

    c. Clean and Fresh

    d. Debt and Payment

17. Choose the synonym pair.

    a. Haste and Deadline

    b. Manuscript and Bible

    c. Feasible and Viable

    d. Priest and Priestess

18. Choose the synonym pair.

    a. Deduct and Induct

    b. Reason and Rationale

    c. Genuine and Congenial

    d. Fraudulent and Errant

19. Choose the synonym pair.

    a. Tinge and Touch

    b. Spot and Dirt

    c. Slur and Narration

    d. Rant and Ask

20. Choose the synonym pair.

    a. Context and Content

    b. Flourish and Colorful

    c. Gist and Summary

    d. Speculate and Witness

21. Choose the synonym pair.

    a. Problem and Solution

    b. Solute and Solvent

    c. Initiate and Instigate

    d. Lament and Joyful

22. Choose the synonym pair.

    a. Expertise and Specialty

    b. Professionalism and Diploma

    c. Accentuate and Articulate

    d. Brazen and Bashful

Choose the synonym of the underlined word.

23. Her <u>amazing</u> talent wowed the audience during the contest.

    a. Ugly

    b. Extraordinary

    c. Plain

    d. Ordinary

24. Jean was <u>furious</u> when her little brother destroyed her favorite doll.

    a. Happy

    b. Lonely

    c. Angry

    d. Surprised

Practice Test Questions 2

25. We will <u>inquire</u> about our scores on the pop quiz.

    a. Ask

    b. Complain

    c. Suggest

    d. Command

26. The car accident was an <u>awful</u> experience the victims want to forget.

    a. Terrible

    b. Pleasant

    c. Wonderful

    d. Unforgettable

27. Cinderella's <u>wicked</u> stepmother failed in the end.

    a. Understanding

    b. Happy

    c. Evil

    d. Supportive

28.

All colonels are officers.
All officers are soldiers.
No colonels are soldiers.

If the first 2 statements are true, then the third statement is:

True   False   Uncertain

29.

No houses on Appleby Street or Francisco streets cost more than $500,000. My house is not on Appleby or Francisco Street.
My house does not cost more than $500,000.

If the first 2 statements are true, then the third statement is:

True   False   Uncertain

30.

Some tropical fish are very sensitive.
I have many types of tropical fish. Some of my fish are very sensitive.

If the first 2 statements are true, then the third statement is:

True   False   Uncertain

31.

Most people in oil producing countries are rich.
I live in an oil producing country.
I am rich.

If the first 2 statements are true, then the third statement is:

True   False   Uncertain

32.

Science can explain all events. Making a decision is an event. Science cannot explain how I make a decision.

If the first 2 statements are true, then the third statement is:

True   False   Uncertain

33.

Doctors can sometimes predict epidemics.
Bird Flu is becoming an epidemic. Doctors know where bird flu will spread.

If the first 2 statements are true, then the third statement is:

True   False   Uncertain

34.

That store sells new and used books.
My textbook is used.
My textbook came from that store.

If the first 2 statements are true, then the third statement is:

True   False   Uncertain

35. Which does not belong?

a. Plate
b. Spoon
c. Dish
d. Dinner

36. Which does not belong?

a. Moon
b. Venus
c. Neptune
d. Saturn

37. Which does not belong?

a. Cat
b. Lion
c. Tiger
d. Fox

38. Which does not belong?

a. Tree
b. Garden
c. Bush
d. Shrub

39. Which does not belong?

a. Grass
b. Flowers
c. Lawn
d. Weeds

Choose the word that completes the relationship.

40. Beautiful : Attractive Powerful : _____

    a. Influential

    b. Poor

    c. Deprived

    d. Gorgeous

41. Chaos : Order :: Reckless : _____

    a. Bitter

    b. Grief

    c. Joy

    d. Careful

42. Servant : Master :: Predator : _____

    a. Nurse

    b. Pupil

    c. Prey

    d. Utensil

43. Winner : Champion :: Sheen : _____

    a. Shimmer

    b. Dark

    c. Sweet

    d. Garbage

44. Pal : Friend :: Enemy : _____

    a. Relative

    b. Business

    c. Foe

    d. Career

45. Strange : Odd :: Offbeat : _____

    a. Melody

    b. Guitar

    c. Drums

    d. Unconventional

46. Frog : Amphibian :: Snake : _____

    a. Reptile

    b. Protozoan

    c. Mammals

    d. Bacteria

47. Color : Red :: Shape : _____

    a. Yellow

    b. Black

    c. Triangle

    d. Hard

48. Clothes : Skirt :: Planets : _____

    a. Comets

    b. Galaxy

    c. Mars

    d. Clouds

49. Fat : Obese :: Brilliant : _____

    a. Glowing

    b. Robust

    c. Intelligent

    d. Poor

50. Bland : Plain :: Broken : _____

    a. Fixed

    b. Busted

    c. Creative

    d. Glass

51. Two : Binary :: Work : _____

    a. Occupation

    b. Vocation

    c. Street

    d. Challenge

52. Botanist : Plants :: Zoologist : _____

    a. Rocks

    b. Planets

    c. Animals

    d. Shells

53. Choose the antonym pair.

    a. Perception and Belief

    b. Fixed and Indefinite

    c. Signal and Symbol

    d. Appearance and Look

54. Choose the antonym pair.

    a. Stratify and Categorize

    b. Plan and Scheme

    c. Strategic and Unplanned

    d. Confused and Mistaken

55. Select the antonym of authentic.

a. Real

b. Imitation

c. Apparition

d. Dream

56. Select the antonym of villain.

a. Actor

b. Actress

c. Antagonist

d. Hero

57. Select the antonym of vanish.

a. Appear

b. Lose

c. Reflection

d. Empty

58. Select the antonym of literal.

a. Manuscript

b. Writing

c. Figurative

d. Untrue

59. Select the antonym of harsh.

a. Mild

b. Light

c. Bulky

d. Bothersome

60. Select the antonym of splurge.

    a. Spend

    b. Count

    c. Use

    d. Save

Section II – Quantitative Skills

1. Consider the following series: 10, 20, 40, 80. What number should come next?

    a. 150

    b. 120

    c. 90

    d. 160

2. Consider the following series: 18395, 18295, 18195, 18095. What number should come next?

    a. 18000

    b. 18950

    c. 17995

    d. 17905

3. Consider the following series: -45, -39, -33, -27. What number should come next?

    a. 21

    b. -21

    c. -25

    d. 25

4. Consider the following series: -100, 100, -200, 0, -300. What number should come next?

    a. 0

    b. -200

    c. -100

    d. 100

5. Consider the following series: 2.3, 2.3, 4.6, 12.18. What number should come next?

    a. 24.36

    b. 48.72

    c. 48

    d. 12.19

6. Consider the following series: 3, 9, 11, 33, 36. What number should come next?

    a. 106

    b. 39

    c. 33

    d. 108

7. Consider the following series: 345, 347, 344, 346. What number should come next?

    a. 345

    b. 343

    c. 348

    d. 349

8. Consider the following series: 21, 21, 31, 31, 41, 41. What number should come next?

    a. 51

    b. 50

    c. 61

    d. 31

9. Consider the following series: 14, 17, 22, 29. What number should come next?

    a. 38

    b. -36

    c. -39

    d. 34

10. Consider the following series: 39, 28, 19, 12, 7. What number should come next?

    a. 1

    b. 4

    c. 0

    d. 2

11. Consider the following series: 3, 5, 10, 12, 24. What 2 numbers should come next?

    a. 48, 58

    b. 26, 28

    c. 48, 50

    d. 26, 52

12. Consider the following series: 1000, 992, 984, 976. What 2 numbers should come next?

    a. 968, 961

    b. 967, 960

    c. 968, 960

    d. 970, 964

13. Consider the following series: 0.1, 0.3, 0.9, 2.7. What 2 numbers should come next?

    a. -8.1, -24.3

    b. 8.1, 24.3

    c. 5.4, 10.8

    d. -5.4, -10.8

14. Consider the following series: 32, 16, 8, 4. What 3 numbers should come

next?

    a. 2, 1, 0.5

    b. 2, 0,-2

    c. 0,-4,-8

    d. 2, 1, 0

15. Consider the following series: 3, ..., 17, 24, 31. What is the missing number?

    a. 8

    b. 12

    c. 10

    d. 5

16. Consider the following series: 3, ..., 9, 12, 15. What is the missing number?

    a. 4

    b. 7

    c. 6

    d. 5

17. Consider the following series: 95, 90, ..., 80, 75. What is the missing number?

    a. 87

    b. 85

    c. 86

    d. 80

18. Consider the following series: ..., 75, 65, 60, 50, 45, 35, ... What 2 numbers are missing?

    a. 70, 35

    b. 65, 35

    c. 80, 30

    d. 65, 30

19. Examine (A) and (B) and find the best answer.

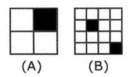

a. The shaded area in (A) is greater than (B)
b. The shaded area in (B) is greater than (A)
c. The shaded area in (A) is equal to (B)

20. Examine (A) and (B) and find the best answer.

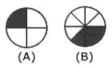

a. The shaded area in (A) is greater than (B)
b. The shaded area in (B) is greater than (A)
c. The shaded area in (A) is equal to (B)

21. Examine (A) and (B) and find the best answer.

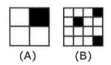

a. The shaded area in (A) is greater than (B)
b. The shaded area in (B) is greater than (A)
c. The shaded area in (A) is equal to (B)

22. **Examine (A) (B) and (C) and find the best answer.**

   a. The shaded area in (A) is equal to (B) and (C).
   b. The shaded area in (C) is less than (A) and (B).
   c. The shaded area in (A) is greater than (B) and (C).
   d. The shaded area in (B) is equal to (A) and (C).

23. **Examine (A) (B) and (C) and find the best answer.**

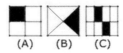

   a. (A) (B) and (C) are equal.
   b. The shaded area in (C) is greater than (A) and (B).
   c. The shaded area in (A) is greater than (B) and (C).
   d. The shaded area in (B) is greater than (A) and (C).

24. **Examine (A) (B) and (C) and find the best answer.**

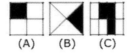

   a. (A) (B) and (C) are equal.
   b. The shaded area in (C) is greater than (A) and (B).
   c. The shaded area in (A) is greater than (B) and (C).
   d. The shaded area in (B) is greater than (A) and (C).

25. **Examine (A) (B) and (C) and find the best answer.**

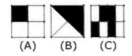

   a. (A) (B) and (C) are equal.
   b. The shaded area in (C) is greater than (A) and (B).
   c. The shaded area in (A) is less than (B) and (C).
   d. The shaded area in (B) is greater than (A) and (C).

26. **Examine (A) (B) and (C) and find the best answer.**

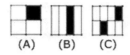

   a. (A) (B) and (C) are equal.
   b. The shaded area in (C) is greater than (A) and (B).
   c. The shaded area in (A) is greater than (B) and (C).
   d. The shaded area in (B) is greater than (A) and (C).

27. **Examine (A) (B) and (C) and find the best answer.**

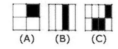

   a. (A) (B) and (C) are equal.
   b. The shaded area in (C) is greater than (A) and (B).
   c. The shaded area in (A) is greater than (B) and (C).
   d. The shaded area in (B) is greater than (A) and (C).

Practice Test Questions 2   153

28. Examine the following and find the best answer.

1. (6 X 1) X (2 X 4)
2. (4 X 7) + (5 X 6)
3. (3 X 4) X (9 - 2)

    a. 2 is the largest

    b. 3 is greater than 1

    c. 1 is greater than 2

    d. None of the Above.

29. Examine the following and find the best answer.

1. 6 X (4 + 3)
2. 4 X (5 X 3)
3. 7 + (3 X 6)

    a. 1 < 2 < 3

    b. 1 < 2 > 3

    c. 2 > 3 > 1

    d. 2 < 3 > 1

30. Examine the following and find the best answer.

1. 50 - (5 X 4)
2. 100 - (6 X 6)
3. 45 - (4 X 2)

    a. 1 < 3 < 2

    b. 1 > 3 > 2

    c. 2 > 1 > 3

    d. 2 < 1 > 3

31. Examine the following and find the best answer.

1. 35 - (6 X 3)
2. 100 - (6 X 10)
3. 75 - (4 X 7)

    a. 1 < 3 < 2

    b. 1 > 3 > 2

c. 2 > 1 > 3
d. 2 < 1 > 3

32. Examine the following and find the best answer.

1. 4 X (2 + 3)
2. 5 X (7 X 3)
3. 9 + (3 X 7)

    a. 3 < 2 > 1
    b. 1 > 2 < 3
    c. 2 > 3 < 1
    d. 2 < 3 < 1

33. Examine the following and find the best answer.

(4 X 3) X (3 X 7)
(7 X 5) + (2 X 5)
(4 X 3) X (7 - 2)

    a. 1 > 2 > 3
    b. 2 > 1 > 3
    c. 3 < 2 < 1
    d. 2 < 1 < 3

34. Examine the following and find the best answer.

1. 12 + (5 X 3)
2. 15 - (9 + 4)
3. 4 + (2 X 9)

    a. 1 > 2 > 3
    b. 2 < 1 > 3
    c. 3 < 2 < 1
    d. 2 < 1 < 3

35. Examine the following and find the best answer.

1. 15 X 6
2. 37 X 5
3. 24 X 2

a. 1 = 3

b. 1 = 2

c. 1 > 2 > 3

d. 3 < 1 < 2

36. Examine the following and find the best answer.

1. (6 X 4) - 5
2. (2 X 8) - 3
3. (3 X 5) – 8

a. 1 and 3 are equal

b. 1 and 3 are not equal

c. 1 and 2 are equal

d. 2 and 3 are equal

37. 2/3 of what number added to 10 is 3 times 15?

a. 50

b. 52.5

c. 65

d. 72.8

38. What number is 25 more than 1/3 of 27?

a. 34

b. -16

c. 20

d. 18

39. What number is 10 less than 5 squared?

a. 25

b. 10

c. 15

d. 40

40. What is 12 more than 3/4 of 40?

    a. 42
    b. 35
    c. 52
    d. 18

41. What is 25 more than 30% of 120?

    a. 75
    b. 50
    c. 65
    d. 35

42. What number subtracted from 75 leaves 15 more than 3/5 of 75?

    a. 25
    b. 15
    c. 30
    d. 12

43. What number divided by 5 is 2/3 of 100?

    a. 333.33
    b. 444.44
    c. 250
    d. 100

44. 1/2 of what number is 9 times 5?

    a. 60
    b. 120
    c. 90
    d. 45

45. What number multiplied by 8 is 10 less than 58?

    a. 5

b. 6
c. 7
d. 8

46. What number subtracted from 25 is 1/5 of 40?

    a. 22
    b. 17
    c. 34
    d. 12

47. What number is 1 less than 1/4 of 16?

    a. 1
    b. 2
    c. 3
    d. 4

48. 1/2 of what number is 8 times 7?

    a. 60
    b. 120
    c. 112
    d. 45

49. What number multiplied by 10 is 15 less than 65?

    a. 5
    b. 6
    c. 7
    d. 8

50. What number subtracted from 25 is 1/5 of 60?

    a. 22
    b. 13
    c. 34
    d. 12

Practice Test Questions 2

Section III - Reading

Questions 1 - 4 refer to the following passage.

Passage 1 - The Respiratory System

The respiratory system's function is to allow oxygen exchange through all parts of the body. The anatomy or structure of the exchange system, and the uses of the exchanged gases, varies depending on the organism. In humans and other mammals, for example, the anatomical features of the respiratory system include airways, lungs, and the respiratory muscles. Molecules of oxygen and carbon dioxide are passively exchanged, by diffusion, between the gaseous external environment and the blood. This exchange occurs in the alveolar region of the lungs.

Other animals, such as insects, have respiratory systems with very simple anatomical features, and in amphibians even the skin plays a vital role in gas exchange. Plants also have respiratory systems but the direction of gas exchange can be opposite to that of animals.

The respiratory system can also be divided into physiological, or functional, zones. These include the conducting zone (the region for gas transport from the outside atmosphere to just above the alveoli), the transitional zone, and the respiratory zone (the alveolar region where gas exchange occurs). [9]

1. What can we infer from the first paragraph in this passage?

a. Human and mammal respiratory systems are the same.

b. The lungs are an important part of the respiratory system.

c. The respiratory system varies in different mammals.

d. Oxygen and carbon dioxide are passive exchanged by the respiratory system.

2. What is the process by which molecules of oxygen and carbon dioxide are passively exchanged?

a. Transfusion

b. Affusion

c. Diffusion

d. Respiratory confusion

3. What organ plays an important role in gas exchange in amphibians?

    a. The skin

    b. The lungs

    c. The gills

    d. The mouth

4. What are the three physiological zones of the respiratory system?

    a. Conducting, transitional, respiratory zones

    b. Redacting, transitional, circulatory zones

    c. Conducting, circulatory, inhibiting zones

    d. Transitional, inhibiting, conducting zones

Questions 5 - 8 refer to the following passage.

ABC Electric Warranty

ABC Electric Company warrants that its products are free from defects in material and workmanship. Subject to the conditions and limitations set forth below, ABC Electric will, at its option, either repair or replace any part of its products that prove defective due to improper workmanship or materials.

This limited warranty does not cover any damage to the product from improper installation, accident, abuse, misuse, natural disaster, insufficient or excessive electrical supply, abnormal mechanical or environmental conditions, or any unauthorized disassembly, repair, or modification.

This limited warranty also does not apply to any product on which the original identification information has been altered, or removed, has not been handled or packaged correctly, or has been sold as second-hand.

This limited warranty covers only repair, replacement, refund or credit for defective ABC Electric products, provided above.

5. I tried to repair my ABC Electric blender, but could not, so can I get it repaired under this warranty?

    a. Yes, the warranty still covers the blender.

b. No, the warranty does not cover the blender.

c. Uncertain. ABC Electric may or may not cover repairs under this warranty.

6. My ABC Electric fan is not working. Will ABC Electric provide a new one or repair this one?

a. ABC Electric will repair my fan

b. ABC Electric will replace my fan

c. ABC Electric could either replace or repair my fan or I can request either a replacement or a repair.

7. My stove was damaged in a flood. Does this warranty cover my stove?

a. Yes, it is covered.

b. No, it is not covered.

c. It may or may not be covered.

d. ABC Electric will decide if it is covered.

8. Which of the following is an example of improper workmanship?

a. Missing parts

b. Defective parts

c. Scratches on the front

d. None of the above

Questions 9 – 11 refer to the following passage.

Passage 3 – Mythology

The main characters in myths are usually gods or supernatural heroes. As sacred stories, rulers and priests have traditionally endorsed their myths and as a result, myths have a close link with religion and politics. In the society where a myth originates, the natives believe the myth is a true account of the remote past. In fact, many societies have two categories of traditional narrative—(1) "true stories," or myths, and (2) "false stories," or fables.

Myths generally take place during a primordial age, when the world was still young, before achieving its current form. These stories explain how the world gained its current form and why the culture developed its customs, institutions, and taboos. Closely related to myth are legend and folktale. Myths, legends, and folktales are different types of traditional stories. Unlike myths, folktales can take place at any time and any place, and the natives do not usually consider them true or sacred. Legends, on the other hand, are similar to myths in that many people have traditionally considered them true. Legends take place in a more recent time, when the world was much as it is today. In addition, legends generally feature humans as their main characters, whereas myths have super-human characters. [10]

9. We can infer from this passage that

a. Folktales took place in a time far past, before civilization covered the earth.

b. Humankind uses myth to explain how the world was created.

c. Myths revolve around gods or supernatural beings; the local community usually accepts these stories as not true.

d. The only difference between a myth and a legend is the time setting of the story.

10. The main purpose of this passage is

a. To distinguish between many types of traditional stories, and explain the background of some traditional story categories.

b. To determine whether myths and legends might be true accounts of history.

c. To show the importance of folktales how these traditional stories made life more bearable in harder times.

d. None of the Above.

11. How are folktales different from myths?

a. Folktales and myth are the same.

b. Folktales are not true and generally not sacred and take place any-time.

c. Myths are not true and generally not sacred and take place anytime.

d. Folktales explained the formation of the world and myths do not.

Questions 12 - 15 refer to the following passage.

Passage 4 – Myths, Legend and Folklore

Cultural historians draw a distinction between myth, legend and folktale simply as a way to group traditional stories. However, in many cultures, drawing a sharp line between myths and legends is not that simple. Instead of dividing their traditional stories into myths, legends, and folktales, some cultures divide them into two categories. The first category roughly corresponds to folktales, and the second is one that combines myths and legends. Similarly, we cannot always separate myths from folktales. One society might consider a story true, making it a myth. Another society may believe the story is fiction, which makes it a folktale. In fact, when a myth loses its status as part of a religious system, it often takes on traits more typical of folktales, with its formerly divine characters now appearing as human heroes, giants, or fairies. Myth, legend, and folktale are only a few of the categories of traditional stories. Other categories include anecdotes and some kinds of jokes. Traditional stories, in turn, are only one category within the larger category of folklore, which also includes items such as gestures, costumes, and music. [10]

12. The main idea of this passage is that

a. Myths, fables, and folktales are not the same thing, and each describes a specific type of story.

b. Traditional stories can be categorized in different ways by different people.

c. Cultures use myths for religious purposes, and when this is no longer true, the people forget and discard these myths.

d. Myths can never become folk tales, because one is true, and the other is false.

13. The terms myth and legend are

a. Categories that are synonymous with true and false.

b. Categories that group traditional stories according to certain characteristics.

c. Interchangeable, because both terms mean a story that is passed down from generation to generation.

d. Meant to distinguish between a story that involves a hero and a cultural message and a story meant only to entertain.

14. Traditional story categories not only include myths and legends, but

a. Can also include gestures, since some cultures passed these down before the written and spoken word.

b. In addition, folklore refers to stories involving fables and fairy tales.

c. These story categories can also include folk music and traditional dress.

d. Traditional stories themselves are a part of the larger category of folklore, which may also include costumes, gestures, and music.

15. This passage shows that

a. There is a distinct difference between a myth and a legend, although both are folktales.

b. Myths are folktales, but folktales are not myths.

c. Myths, legends, and folktales play an important part in tradition and the past, and are a rich and colorful part of history.

d. Most cultures consider myths to be true.

Questions 16 - 19 refer to the following passage.

Passage 5 – Ways Characters Communicate in Theater

Playwrights give their characters voices in a way that gives depth and added meaning to what happens on stage during their play. There are different types of speech in scripts that allow characters to talk with themselves, with other characters, and even with the audience.

It is very unique to theater that characters may talk "to themselves." When characters do this, the speech they give is called a soliloquy. Soliloquies are usually poetic, introspective, moving, and can tell audience members about the feelings, motivations, or suspicions of an individual character without that character having to reveal them to other characters on stage. "To be or not to be" is a famous soliloquy given by Hamlet as he considers difficult but important themes, such as life and death.

The most common type of communication in plays is when one character is speaking to another or a group of other characters. This is generally called dialogue, but can also be called monologue if one character speaks without being interrupted for a long time. It is not necessarily the most important type of communication, but it is the most common because the plot of the play cannot really progress without it.

Lastly, and most unique to theater (although it has been used somewhat in film) is when a character speaks directly to the audience. This is called an aside, and scripts usually specifically direct actors to do this. Asides are usually comical, an inside joke between the character and the audience, and very short. The actor will usually face the audience when delivering them, even if it's for a moment, so the audience can recognize this move as an aside.

All three of these types of communication are important to the art of theater, and have been perfected by famous playwrights like Shakespeare. Understanding these types of communication can help an audience member grasp what is artful about the script and action of a play.

16. According to the passage, characters in plays communicate to

    a. move the plot forward.

    b. show the private thoughts and feelings of one character.

    c. make the audience laugh.

    d. add beauty and artistry to the play.

17. When Hamlet delivers "To be or not to be," he can most likely be described as

    a. solitary

    b. thoughtful

    c. dramatic

    d. hopeless

18. The author uses parentheses to punctuate "although it has been used somewhat in film"

    a. to show that films are less important

    b. instead of using commas so that the sentence is not interrupted

    c. because parenthesis help separate details that are not as important

    d. to show that films are not as artistic

19. It can be understood that by the phrase "give their characters voices," the author means that

    a. playwrights are generous.

    b. playwrights are changing the sound or meaning of characters' voices to fit what they had in mind.

    c. dialogue is important in creating characters.

    d. playwrights may be the parent of one of their actors and literally give them their voice.

Practice Test Questions 2

Questions 20 - 23 refer to the following passage.

Passage 6 – Trees II

With an estimated 100,000 species, trees represent 25 percent of all living plant species. Most tree species grow in tropical regions of the world and many of these areas have not been surveyed by botanists, making species diversity poorly understood. The earliest trees were tree ferns and horsetails, which grew in forests in the Carboniferous period. Tree ferns still survive, but the only surviving horsetails are no longer in tree form. Later, in the Triassic period, conifers and ginkgos, appeared, followed by flowering plants after that in the Cretaceous period. [11]

20. Do botanists understand the number of tree species?

    a. Yes botanists know exactly how many tree species there are

    b. No, the species diversity is not well understood

    c. Yes, botanists are sure

    d. No, botanists have no idea

21. Where do most trees species grow?

    a. Most tree species grow in tropical regions.

    b. There is no one area where most tree species grow.

    c. Tree species grow in 25% of the world.

    d. There are 100,000 tree species.

22. What tree(s) survived from the Carboniferous period?

    a. 25% of all trees

    b. Horsetails

    c. Conifers

    d. Tree Ferns

23. Choose the correct list below, ranked from oldest to youngest trees.

    a. Flowering plants, conifers and ginkgos, tree ferns and horsetails.

    b. Tree ferns and horsetails, conifers and ginkgos, flowering plants.

    c. Tree ferns and horsetails, flowering plants, conifers and ginkgos.

    d. Conifers and ginkgos, tree ferns and horsetails, flowering plants.

Questions 24 - 26 refer to the following passage.

Lowest Price Guarantee

Get it for less. Guaranteed!

ABC Electric will beat any advertised price by 10% of the difference.

1) If you find a lower advertised price, we will beat it by 10% of the difference.

2) If you find a lower advertised price within 30 days* of your purchase we will beat it by 10% of the difference.

3) If our own price is reduced within 30 days* of your purchase, bring in your receipt and we will refund the difference.

*14 days for computers, monitors, printers, laptops, tablets, cellular & wireless devices, home security products, projectors, camcorders, digital cameras, radar detectors, portable DVD players, DJ and pro-audio equipment, and air conditioners.

24. I bought a radar detector 15 days ago and saw an ad for the same model only cheaper. Can I get 10% of the difference refunded?

    a. Yes. Since it is less than 30 days, you can get 10% of the difference re-funded.

    b. No. Since it is more than 14 days, you cannot get 10% of the difference re-funded.

    c. It depends on the cashier.

    d. Yes. You can get the difference refunded.

Practice Test Questions 2

25. I bought a flat-screen TV for $500 10 days ago and found an advertisement for the same TV, at another store, on sale for $400. How much will ABC refund under this guarantee?

    a. $100

    b. $110

    c. $10

    d. $400

26. What is the purpose of this passage?

    a. To inform

    b. To educate

    c. To persuade

    d. To entertain

Questions 27 - 29 refer to the following passage.

Passage 8 - Insects

Insects have segmented bodies supported by an exoskeleton, a hard outer covering made mostly of chitin. The segments of the body are organized into three distinctive connected units, a head, a thorax, and an abdomen. The head supports a pair of antennae, a pair of compound eyes, and three sets of appendages that form the mouthparts.

The thorax has six segmented legs and, if present in the species, two or four wings. The abdomen consists of eleven segments, though in a few species these segments may be fused together or very small.

Overall, there are 24 segments. The abdomen also contains most of the digestive, respiratory, excretory and reproductive internal structures. There is considerable variation and many adaptations in the body parts of insects especially wings, legs, antenna and mouthparts. [12]

27. How many units do insects have?

    a. Insects are divided into 24 units.

    b. Insects are divided into 3 units.

    c. Insects are divided into segments not units.

    d. It depends on the species.

28. Which of the following is true?

    a. All insects have 2 wings.

    b. All insects have 4 wings.

    c. Some insects have 2 wings.

    d. Some insects have 2 or 4 wings.

29. What is true of insect's abdomen?

    a. It contains some of the organs.

    b. It is too small for any organs.

    c. It contains all of the organs.

    d. None of the above.

Questions 30 - 33 refer to the following passage.

Passage 9 - Women and Advertising

Only in the last few generations have media messages been so widespread and so readily seen, heard, and read by so many people. Advertising is an important part of both selling and buying anything from soap to cereal to jeans. For whatever reason, more consumers are women than are men. Media message are subtle but powerful, and more attention has been paid lately to how these message affect women.

Of all the products that women buy, makeup, clothes, and other stylistic or cosmetic products are among the most popular. This means that companies focus their advertising on women, promising them that their product will make her feel, look, or smell better than the next company's product will. This competition has resulted in advertising that is more and more ideal and less and less possible for everyday women. However, because women do look to these ideals and the products they represent as how they can potentially become, many women have developed unhealthy attitudes about themselves when they have failed to become those ideals.

In recent years, more companies have tried to change advertisements to be healthier for women. This includes featuring models of more sizes and addressing a huge outcry against unfair tools such as airbrushing and photo editing. There is considerable debate over the right balance between real and ideal is, because fashion is also considered art and some changes are made to elevate purposefully fashionable products and signify that they are creative, innovative, and the work of individual people. Artists want their freedom protected as much as women do, and advertising agencies are often caught in the middle.

Some claim that the companies who make these changes are not doing enough. Many people worry that there are still not enough models of different sizes and different ethnicities. Some people claim that companies use this healthier type of advertisement not for the good of women, but because they would like to sell products to the women who are looking for these kinds of messages. This is also a hard balance to find: companies do need to make money, and women do need to feel respected.

While the focus of this change has been on women, advertising can also affect men, and this change will hopefully be a lesson on media for all consumers.

30. The second paragraph states that advertising focuses on women

    a. to shape what the ideal should be.

    b. because women buy makeup.

    c. because women are easily persuaded.

    d. because of the types of products that women buy.

31. According to the passage, fashion artists and female consumers are at odds because

    a. there is a debate going on and disagreement drives people apart.

    b. both of them are trying to protect their freedom to do something.

    c. artists want to elevate their products above the reach of women.

    d. women are creative, innovative, individual people.

32. The author uses the phrase "for whatever reason" in this passage to

    a. keep the focus of the paragraph on media messages and not on the differences between men and women.

    b. show that the reason for this is unimportant.

    c. argue that it is stupid that more women are consumers than men.

    d. show that he or she is tired of talking about why media messages are important.

33. This passage suggests that

    a. advertising companies are still working on making their messages better.

    b. all advertising companies seek to be more approachable for women.

    c. women are only buying from companies that respect them.

    d. artists could stop producing fashionable products if they feel bullied.

Questions 34 - 37 refer to the following passage.

Passage 10 - FDR, the Treaty of Versailles, and the Fourteen Points

At the conclusion of World War I, those who had won the war and those who were forced to admit defeat welcomed the end of the war and expected that a peace treaty would be signed. The American president, Franklin D. Roosevelt, played an important part in proposing what the agreements should be and did so through his Fourteen Points.

World War I had begun in 1914 when an Austrian archduke was assassinated, leading to a domino effect that pulled the world's most powerful countries into war on a large scale. The war catalyzed the creation and use of deadly weapons that had not previously existed, resulting in a great loss of soldiers on both sides of the fighting. More than 9 million soldiers were killed.

The United States agreed to enter the war right before it ended, and they believed that the decision to become finally involved brought on the end of the war. FDR made it very clear that the U.S. was entering the war for moral reasons and had an agenda focused on world peace. The Fourteen Points were individual goals and ideas (focused on peace, free trade, open communication, and self reliance) that FDR wanted the power nations to strive for now that the war had concluded. He was optimistic and had many ideas about what could be accomplished through, and during the post-war peace. However, FDR's fourteen points were poorly received when he presented them to the leaders of other world powers, many of whom wanted only to help their own countries and to punish the Germans for fueling the war, and they fell by the wayside. World War II was imminent, for Germany lost everything.

Some historians believe that the other leaders who participated in the Treaty of Versailles weren't receptive to the Fourteen Points because World War I was fought almost entirely on European soil, and the United States lost much less than did the other powers. FDR was in a unique position to determine the fate of the war, but doing it on his own terms did not help accomplish his goals. This is only one historical example of how the United State has tried to use its power as an important country, but found itself limited because of geological or ideological factors.

34. The main idea of this passage is that

a. World War I was unfair because no fighting took place in America.

b. World War II happened because of the Treaty of Versailles.

c. the power the United States has to help other countries also prevents it from helping other countries

d. Franklin D. Roosevelt was one of the United States' smartest presidents

35. According to the second paragraph, World War I started because

a. an archduke was assassinated.

b. weapons that were more deadly had been developed.

c. a domino effect of allies agreeing to help each other.

d. the world's most powerful countries were large.

36. The author includes the detail that 9 million soldiers were killed

a. to demonstrate why European leaders were hesitant to accept peace.

b. to show the reader the dangers of deadly weapons.

c. to make the reader think about which countries lost the most soldiers.

d. to demonstrate why World War II was imminent.

37. According to this passage, the word catalyzed means

a. analyzed

b. sped up

c. invented

d. funded

Section III
Part II - Vocabulary

38. Choose the best definition of anecdote.

a. A short account of an incident

b. Something that comes before

c. The use of humour, irony, exaggeration, or ridicule

d. Constant fluctuations

39. Choose the adjective that means shocking, terrible or wicked.

    a. Pleasantries

    b. Heinous

    c. Shrewd

    d. Provencal

40. Choose the noun that means a person or thing that tells or announces the coming of someone or something.

    a. Harbinger

    b. Evasion

    c. Bleak

    d. Craven

41. Choose a word that means the same as the underlined word.

He wasn't especially generous. All the servings were very <u>judicious</u>.

    a. Abundant

    b. Careful

    c. Extravagant

    d. Careless

42. Fill in the blank.

Because of the growing use of _____ as a fuel, corn production has greatly increased.

    a. Alcohol

    b. Ethanol

    c. Natural gas

    d. Oil

Practice Test Questions 2

43. Fill in the blank.

In heavily industrialized areas, the pollution of the air causes many to develop _____ diseases.

  a. Respiratory

  b. Cardiac

  c. Alimentary

  d. Circulatory

44. Choose the best definition of inherent.

  a. To receive money in a will

  b. An essential part of

  c. To receive money from a will

  d. None of the above

45. Choose the best definition of vapid.

  a. adj. tasteless or bland

  b. v. To inflict, as a revenge or punishment

  c. v. to convert into gas

  d. v. to go up in smoke

46. Choose the best definition of waif.

  a. n. a sick and hungry child

  b. n. an orphan staying in a foster home

  c. n. homeless child or stray

  d. n. a type of French bread eaten with cheese

47. Choose the adjective that means similar or identical.

  a. Soluble

  b. Assembly

  c. Conclave

  d. Homologous

48. Choose a word with the same meaning as the underlined word.

We used that operating system 20 years ago, now it is <u>obsolete</u>.

> a. Functional
> b. Disused
> c. Obese
> d. None of the Above

49. Choose the word with the same meaning as the underlined word

His bad manners really <u>rankle</u> me.

> a. Annoy
> b. Obsolete
> c. Enliven
> d. None of the above

50. Fill in the blank.

Because hydroelectric power is a _____ source of energy, its use is excellent for the environment.

> a. Significant
> b. Disposable
> c. Renewable
> d. Reusable

51. Choose the best definition of torpid.

> a. Fast
> b. Rapid
> c. Sluggish
> d. Violent

52. Choose the best definition of gregarious.

a. Sociable

b. Introverted

c. Large

d. Solitary

53. Choose the best definition of mutation.

a. v. To utter with a loud and vehement voice

b. n. change or alteration

c. n. An act or exercise of will

d. v. To cause to be one

54. Choose the best definition of lithe.

a. adj. small in size

b. adj. Artificial

c. adj. flexible or plaint

d. adj. fake

55. Choose the best definition of resent.

a. adj. To express displeasure or indignation

b. v. To cause to be one

c. adj. Clumsy

d. adj. strong feelings of love

56. Choose the adjective that means irrelevant not having substance or matter.

a. Immaterial

b. Prohibition

c. Prediction

d. Brokerage

57. Choose the adjective that means perfect, no faults or errors.

    a. Impeccable

    b. Formidable

    c. Genteel

    d. Disputation

58. Choose the best definition of pudgy.

    a. v. to draw general inferences

    b. Adj. fat, plump and overweight

    c. n. permanence

    d. adj. spoilt or bad condition

59. Choose the best definition of alloy.

    a. To mix with something superior

    b. To mix

    c. To mix with something inferior

    d. To purify

60. Fill in the blank.

The process required the use of highly _____ liquids, so fire extinguishers were everywhere in the factory.

    a. Erratic

    b. Combustible

    c. Stable

    d. Neutral

Section IV – Math

1. The sum of the digits of a 2-digit number is 12. If we switch the digits, the number we get will be greater than the initial one by 36. Find the initial number.

    a. 39
    b. 48
    c. 57
    d. 75

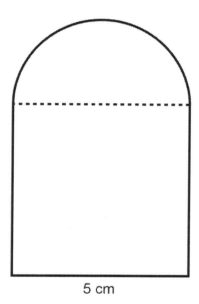

5 cm

Note: Figure not drawn to scale

2. What is the perimeter of the above shape?

    a. 17.5 π cm
    b. 20 π cm
    c. 15 π cm
    d. 25 π cm

3. Kate's father is 32 years older than Kate is. In 5 years, he will be five times older. How old is Kate?

    a. 2

    b. 3

    c. 5

    d. 6

4. If Lynn can type a page in p minutes, what portion of the page can she do in 5 minutes?

    a. 5/p

    b. p - 5

    c. p + 5

    d. p/5

5. If Sally can paint a house in 4 hours, and John can paint the same house in 6 hours, how long will it take for both of them to paint the house together?

    a. 2 hours and 24 minutes

    b. 3 hours and 12 minutes

    c. 3 hours and 44 minutes

    d. 4 hours and 10 minutes

6. The following are the number of people that attended a particular church, every Friday for 7 weeks – 62, 18, 39, 13, 16, 37, 25. Find the average.

    a. 25

    b. 210

    c. 62

    d. 30

7. Sales of a local football team's season tickets have gone up 10% in the current season to 880 tickets. Last year, they sold X season tickets. X equals:

    a. 700

    b. 800

    c. 880

d. 928

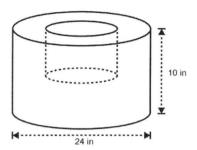

Note: Figure not drawn to scale

8. What is the volume of the above solid made by a hollow cylinder that is half the size (in all dimensions) of the larger cylinder?

    a. 1440 π in³

    b. 1260 π in³

    c. 1040 π in³

    d. 960 π in³

9. Two trains start at the same time in different directions. One travels at an average speed of 72 km/hr., and the other at 52 km/hr. After 20 minutes how far apart are they?

    a. 6.67 km

    b. 17.33 km

    c. 24.3 km

    d. 41.33 km

10. There were some oranges in a basket, by adding 8/5 of these, the total became 130. How many oranges were in the basket before?

    a. 60

    b. 50

    c. 40

    d. 35

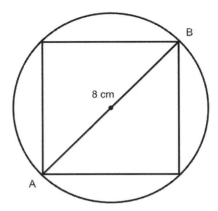

Note: Figure not drawn to scale

11. What is area of the circle?

    a. 4 π cm²

    b. 12 π cm²

    c. 10 π cm²

    d. 16 π cm²

12. John jogs around a 75-meter diameter track 7 times. How much linear distance did he cover?

    a. 1250 meters

    b. 1450 meters

    c. 1650 meters

    d. 1725 meters

13. In an office, 12 employees can finish a task in 7 hours. If two of them are absent, how much more time will they have to work to complete the task?

    a. 10 minutes

    b. 12 minutes

    c. 15 minutes

    d. 20 minutes

14. A bullet train traveling at 300km/hr passes station A at 8:56 pm. What time will the train reach station B, which is 45km away?

    a. 9:03 pm
    b. 9:05 pm
    c. 9:07 pm
    d. 9:10 pm

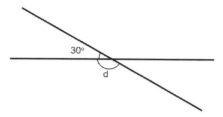

15. What is the indicated angle above?

    a. 150°
    b. 330°
    c. 60°
    d. 120°

16. In an 80 km marathon race, George runs 2 km/hr. faster than Marsha does. George reaches the finish line in 3.2 hrs. At that time, how far is Marsh from finish line?

    a. 6.4 km
    b. 5.6 km
    c. 5.2 km
    d. 4.8 km

17. On a circular jogging track with a circumference of 1.2 km, John, Tony and David walk at the rate of 120, 100 and 75 meters per minute respectively. If they all start walking in the same direction, how long will it take until they are together again?

    a. 200 minutes
    b. 220 minutes
    c. 240 minutes
    d. 260 minutes

18. On a scaled map, city A is 12.4 cm away from city B. If the scale is 1 cm = 5 km then what is the actual distance between these two cities?

    a. 12.4 km

    b. 48.4 km

    c. 58 km

    d. 62 km

19. In a 30-minute test, there are 40 problems. A student solved 28 problems in first 25 minutes. How many seconds should she give to each of the remaining problems?

    a. 20 seconds

    b. 23 seconds

    c. 25 seconds

    d. 27 seconds

Note: Figure not drawn to scale

20. What is the perimeter of the parallelogram above?

    a. 12 cm

    b. 26 cm

    c. 13 cm

    d. (13+x) cm

21. Estimate 2009 x 108.

    a. 110,000

    b. 2,0000

    c. 21,000

    d. 210,000

22. Richard sold 12 shirts for total revenue of $336 at 8% profit. What is the purchase price of each shirt?

    a. $25.76

    b. $24.50

    c. $23.75

    d. $22.50

23. If we know it takes 12 men to operate four machines, how many are required to operate 20 machines?

    a. 6

    b. 20

    c. 60

    d. 9

24. The playing times for three songs on a compact disc are: 4 minutes 56 seconds for song A, 2 minutes 30 seconds for song B, 10 minutes 16 seconds for song C. What's the average playing time for the three songs?

    a. 17 minutes 42 seconds

    b. 6 minutes 7 seconds

    c. 6 minutes

    d. 5 minutes 54 seconds

25. John is a barber and receives 40% of the amount paid by his customers, and all of the tips. If a customer pays $8.50 for a haircut and leaves a tip of $1.30, how much money does John receive?

    a. $3.92

    b. $4.70

    c. $5.30

    d. $6.40

26. A company paid a total of $2850 to book 6 single rooms and 4 double rooms in a hotel for one night. Another company paid $3185 to book for 13 single rooms for one night in the same hotel. What is the cost for single and double rooms in that hotel?

    a. Single $250, double $345

    b. Single $254, double $350

    c. single $245, double $305

    d. single $245, double $345

27. The length of a rectangle is 5 in. more than its width. The perimeter of the rectangle is 26 in. What is the width and length of the rectangle?

    a. Width 6 in., Length 9 in.

    b. Width 4 in., Length 9 in.

    c. Width 4 in., Length 5 in.

    d. Width 6 in., Length 11 in.

28. A basket contains 125 oranges, mangos and apples. If 3/5 of the fruits in the basket are mangos, and only 2/5 of the mangos are ripe, how many ripe mangos are there in the basket?

    a. 30

    b. 68

    c. 55

    d. 47

29. Calculate (3a + 4b) * d when A = 2, b = 4 and d = 8

    a. 40

    b. 150

    c. 112

    d. 176

30. c = 4, n = 5 and x = 3. Calculate 2cnx/2n

    a. 12

    b. 50

    c. 8

    d. 21

31. Simplify 3 1/2 / 2 4/5

    a. 1 1/4

    b. 2 1/4

    c. 1 1/3

    d. 2 1/3

32. Solve 2b/3 + 3a/5 – 2, where b = 9 and a = 10

    a. 5

    b. 10

    c. 20

    d. 9

33. Simplify (1/3 + 2/6) - (3/4 - 1/3)

    a. 1/4

    b. 5/11

    c. 3/7

    d. 2/9

34. Simplify (4/5 - 3/10) + (2/3 – 3/9) =

    a. 4/11

    b. 11/15

    c. 7/15

    d. 9/11

35. Translate the following into an equation: 2 + a number divided by 7.

    a. (2 + X)/7
    b. (7 + X)/2
    c. (2 + 7)/X
    d. 2/(7 + X)

36. If a = 12 and b = 8, solve 6b - a + 2a

    a. 12/9
    b. 18
    c. 16
    d. 12

37. Simplify 3 2/3 - 1 2/8

    a. 3/5
    b. 3/5
    c. 2 5/12
    d. 5/12

38. Simplify 7 2/5 – 4 3/10

    a. 3 1/10
    b. 3 2/5
    c. 4 1/5
    d. 3 7/10

39. Solve for x. -4 – 5x = 8x + 8

    a. 6
    b. 3
    c. 4
    d. 2

40. Solve 2 1/3 x 1 3/7 x 3/4

    a. 2 1/2
    b. 9
    c. 3 2/3
    d. 2 2/5

41. Simplify 7 4/5 – 4 2/3

    a. 4 2/5
    b. 3 2/15
    c. 3 7/15
    d. 4 3/5

42. Solve for x. 12x - 8 = 3x + 10

    a. 6
    b. 4
    c. 2
    d. 3

43. Simplify (3/5 - 2/5) + (3/4 – 2/8)

    a. 18/45
    b. 7/11
    c. 9/20
    d. 12/19

44. Solve for a. 6a + 4 = 28 + 2a

    a. 4
    b. 8
    c. 2
    d. 6

45. Simplify (3/4 - 1/4) - (3/5 – 2/5)

    a. 9/20
    b. 4/15
    c. 7/15
    d. 11/20

46. Solve for x. 6 + 9x = 12 + 7x

    a. 5
    b. 2
    c. 4
    d. 3

47. Simplify 6 2/5 / 2 2/7

    a. 2 1/4
    b. 1 1/5
    c. 2 4/5
    d. 2 2/3

48. Solve for a. -6 + 7a = 9 + 4a

    a. 3
    b. 5
    c. 2
    d. 6

49. Simplify 2 1/3 / 1 2/5

    a. 1 2/5
    b. 1 2/3
    c. 1 1/7
    d. 2 2/5

50. 2/3 x 1 4/7 x 5 1/4

    a. 3 1/4
    b. 5 1/2
    c. 6 2/3
    d. 4 2/5

51. Simplify 4 1/5 / 2 1/3

    a. 1 4/5
    b. 2 1/4
    c. 1 3/7
    d. 2 1/4

52. 10/3 x 2 1/4 x 3 1/5

    a. 1 3/4
    b. 24
    c. 7 2/7
    d. 5 1/5

53. Simplify 3 1/9 / 2 2/3

    a. 2 1/5
    b. 2 3/4
    c. 1 1/6
    d. 1 1/4

54. What is -9 + (+6) − (-2)

    a. -3
    b. 1
    c. -1
    d. -5

55. Simplify 5 1/2 – 5 3/7

    a. 1/10

    b. 1/14

    c. 1/7

    d. 2/7

56. What is -3 - (-7) - (+5)?

    a. -6

    b. 6

    c. 3

    d. -1

57. Solve 3 3/4 x 4/5 x 1 3/4

    a. 3 3/4

    b. 4 1/3

    c. 6

    d. 5 1/4

58. Simplify 6 3/5 – 4 4/5

    a. 2 4/5

    b. 2 3/5

    c. 2 9/5

    d. 1 1/5

59. Estimate 46,227 + 101,032.

    a. 14,700

    b. 147,000

    c. 14,700,000

    d. 104,700

60. Solve √121

    a. 11

    b. 12

    c. 21

    d. None of the above

Section V – Language Arts

1. Choose the sentence below with the correct punctuation.

    a. There are many species of owls, the Great-Horned Owl, the Snowy Owl, and the Western Screech Owl, and the Barn Owl.

    b. There are many species of owls, the Great-Horned Owl: the Snowy Owl: and the Western Screech Owl, and the Barn Owl.

    c. There are many species of owls: the Great-Horned Owl, the Snowy Owl, and the Western Screech Owl, and the Barn Owl.

    d. There are many species of owls: the Great-Horned Owl, the Snowy Owl, and the Western Screech Owl, and the Barn Owl.

2. Choose the sentence below with the correct punctuation.

    a. In his most famous speech, Reverend King proclaimed: "I have a dream!"

    b. In his most famous speech, Reverend King proclaimed; "I have a dream!"

    c. In his most famous speech, Reverend King proclaimed. "I have a dream!"

    d. In his most famous speech: Reverend King proclaimed, "I have a dream!"

3. Choose the sentence below with the correct punctuation.

    a. Puzzled — Joe said, "You aren't going to pay me until ?"

    b. Puzzled, Joe said, "You aren't going to pay me until ?"

    c. Puzzled, Joe said, "You aren't going to pay me until —?"

    d. Puzzled, Joe said, "You aren't going to pay me until, ?"

4. Choose the sentence below with the correct punctuation.

a. The years of his employment were not consecutive, being from 1999 to 2001 and 2002 – 2004.

b. The years of his employment were not consecutive, being from 1999 – 2001 and 2002 – 2004.

c. The years of his employment were not consecutive, being from 1999 _ 2001   and 2002_ 2004.

d. The years of his employment were not consecutive, being from 1999, 2001 and 2002, 2004.

5. Which sentence uses the period correctly?

a. Henry VIII

b. Henry VIII

c. Pope John XXIII

d. Vol. IV

6. Choose the correct answer.

a. Ph.D.

b. BSN.

c. N.A.S.A.

d. F.B.I.

7. Sit up straight _____

a. ;

b. ?

c. .

d. :

8. Choose the sentence with the correct capitalization.

a. The Pharmalife Drugstore is on the north corner.

b. The Pharmalife Drugstore is on the North corner.

c. The pharmalife drugstore is on the north corner.

d. None of the above.

9. Choose the sentence with the correct capitalization.

a. The motto of The New York times is "All The News That's Fit to Print."

b. The Motto of The New York Times is "All The News That's Fit to Print."

c. The motto of The New York Times is "All The News That's Fit to Print."

d. The motto of The New York Times is "All the News That's Fit to Print."

10. Choose the sentence with the correct capitalization.

a. During the years he was President, the country fought two wars.

b. During the years he was president, the country fought two wars.

c. During the years he was president, the Country fought two wars.

d. During the years he was President, the Country fought two wars.

11. Choose the sentence with the correct capitalization.

a. Shakespeare wrote more than 37 Plays, including Much Ado about Nothing.

b. Shakespeare wrote more than 37 plays, including Much ado about nothing.

c. Shakespeare wrote more than 37 plays, including Much Ado about Nothing.

d. None of the above.

12. Choose the sentence with the correct capitalization.

a. George forgot to call his Grandmother and Aunt Sue during the holidays.

b. George forgot to call his Grandmother and Aunt Sue during the Holidays.

c. George forgot to call his grandmother and Aunt Sue during the holidays.

d. George forgot to call his grandmother and aunt Sue during the holidays.

13. Choose the sentence with the correct capitalization.

a. The Sahara Desert is found in the northern part of Africa.

b. The Sahara Desert is found in the Northern part of Africa.

c. The Sahara desert is found in the northern part of Africa.

d. The Sahara desert is found in the Northern part of Africa.

14. Choose the sentence with the correct capitalization.

a. The State of Georgia is located south of North Carolina.

b. The state of Georgia is located South of North Carolina.

c. The state of Georgia is located south of north Carolina.

d. The state of Georgia is located south of North Carolina.

15. Choose the sentence with the correct capitalization.

a. The best known rivers in China are the Yangtze river, the Yellow river, and the Pearl river.

b. The best known Rivers in China are the Yangtze River, the Yellow River, and the Pearl River.

c. The best known rivers in China are the Yangtze River, the Yellow River, and the Pearl River.

d. The best known Rivers in China are the Yangtze river, the Yellow river, and the Pearl river.

16. Choose the sentence with the correct capitalization.

a. The abbreviation of the American medical association is the AMA.

b. The abbreviation of the american medical association is the AMA.

c. The abbreviation of the American Medical Association is the AMA.

d. The abbreviation of the American medical Association is the AMA.

17. Choose the sentence with the correct capitalization.

a. Mrs. Jones is my English teacher, but I have Mr. Brown for Science and mathematics.

b. Mrs. Jones is my English teacher, but I have Mr. Brown for Science and Mathematics.

c. Mrs. Jones is my english teacher, but I have Mr. Brown for science and mathematics.

d. Mrs. Jones is my English teacher, but I have Mr. Brown for science and mathematics.

Practice Test Questions 2   *197*

18. Choose the sentence with the correct capitalization.

a. That country was ruled by a Dictator for decades, but recently, its people elected their first president.

b. That country was ruled by a dictator for decades, but recently, its people elected their first President.

c. That country was ruled by a dictator for decades, but recently, its people elected their first president.

d. That country was ruled by a Dictator for decades, but recently, its people elected their first President.

19. Choose the sentence with the correct usage.

a. Vegetables are a healthy food; eating them can make you more healthful.

b. Vegetables are a healthful food; eating them can make you more healthful.

c. Vegetables are a healthy food; eating them can make you more healthy.

d. Vegetables are a healthful food; eating them can make you more healthy.

20. Choose the sentence with the correct usage.

a. When James went into his room, he found that his clothes had been put in the closet.

b. When James went in his room, he found that his clothes had been put in the closet.

c. When James went into his room, he found that his clothes had been put into the closet.

d. When James went in his room, he found that his clothes had been put into the closet.

21. Choose the sentence with the correct usage.

a. After you lay the books on the counter, you may lay down for a nap.

b. After you lie the books on the counter, you may lay down for a nap.

c. After you lay the books on the counter, you may lie down for a nap.

d. After you lay the books on the counter, you may lay down for a nap.

22. Choose the sentence with the correct usage.

a. Once the chickens had layed their eggs, they lay on their nests to hatch them.

b. Once the chickens had lay their eggs, they lay on their nests to hatch them.

c. Once the chickens had laid their eggs, they lay on their nests to hatch them.

d. Once the chickens had laid their eggs, they laid on their nests to hatch them.

23. Choose the sentence with the correct usage.

a. Mrs. Foster taught me many things, but I learned the most from Mr. Wallace.

b. Mrs. Foster learned me many things, but I was taught the most by Mr. Wallace.

c. Mrs. Foster learned me many things, but I learned the most from Mr. Wallace.

d. Mrs. Foster taught me many things, but I taught the most from Mr. Wallace.

24. Choose the sentence with the correct usage.

a. He did not have to loose the race; if only his shoes weren't so lose!

b. He did not have to lose the race; if only his shoes weren't so loose!

c. He did not have to loose the race; if only his shoes weren't so lose!

d. He did not have to lose the race; if only his shoes weren't so lose!

25. Choose the sentence with the correct usage.

a. The attorney did not want to prosecute the defendant; his goal was to prosecute the guilty party.

b. The attorney did not want to persecute the defendant; his goal was to persecute the guilty party.

c. The attorney did not want to prosecute the defendant; his goal was to persecute the guilty party.

d. The attorney did not want to persecute the defendant; his goal was to prosecute the guilty party.

26. Choose the sentence with the correct usage.

a. The speeches must precede the election; the election cannot proceed without hearing from the candidates.

b. The speeches must precede the election; the election cannot precede without hearing from the candidates.

c. The speeches must proceed the election; the election cannot precede without hearing from the candidates.

d. The speeches must proceed the election; the election cannot proceed without hearing from the candidates.

27. Choose the sentence with the correct usage.

a. Before a lawyer can rise an objection, he must first rise to his feet.

b. Before a lawyer can raise an objection, he must first raise to his feet.

c. Before a lawyer can raise an objection, he must first rise to his feet.

d. Before a lawyer can rise an objection, he must first raise to his feet.

28. Choose the sentence with the correct usage.

a. You shouldn't sit in that chair wearing black pants; I set the white cat there just a moment ago.

b. You shouldn't set in that chair wearing black pants; I sit the white cat there just a moment ago.

c. You shouldn't set in that chair wearing black pants; I set the white cat there just a moment ago.

d. You shouldn't sit in that chair wearing black pants; I sit the white cat there just a moment ago.

For each of the sentences below choose the correct word to replace the underlined word or phrase.

29. Sarah bought some stationeries.

a. stationary

b. stationarys

c. stationaryes

d. None of the Above

30. He is a man of his words.

    a. wordy

    b. word

    c. wordes

    d. None of the Above

31. I have two son in laws.

    a. sons in laws.

    b. sons on law.

    c. sons in law.

    d. None of the Above.

32. We'll go to the beach in our vacation.

    a. on

    b. at

    c. from

    d. None of the Above.

33. We'll go to the beach during the summer vocations.

    a. summer vacation

    b. summer's vacation

    c. summer vocation

    d. summers vacation

34. Richard is the tallest of the two boys.

    a. tall

    b. taller

    c. taller than

    d. None of the Above.

35. Choose the correct spelling.

a. lighting
b. lightning
c. lightining
d. lightming

36. Choose the correct spelling.

a. occasionaly
b. occassionally
c. occasionally
d. ocasionally

37. Choose the correct spelling.

a. pronounciation
b. pronuonciation
c. pronounciation
d. pronunciation

38. Choose the correct spelling.

a. questionnaire
b. questionnare
c. questionaire
d. questionare

39. Choose the correct spelling.

a. sergeant
b. sergent
c. sergant
d. sergernt

40. Choose the correct spelling.

    a. immeadiately

    b. imeddiately

    c. immediately

    d. immedaitely

41. Choose the correct spelling.

    a. vacume

    b. vaccum

    c. vacum

    d. vacuum

42. Choose the correct spelling.

    a. theshold

    b. treshold

    c. threshold

    d. threeshold

43. Choose the correct spelling.

    a. segie

    b. sigie

    c. seige

    d. siege

44. Choose the correct spelling.

    a. supersede

    b. supercede

    c. superseed

    d. supercede

45. Choose the correct spelling.

a. rhytm

b. rythym

c. rhythm

d. ryhtym

46. Choose the correct spelling.

a. thourough

b. thoruogh

c. thourogh

d. thorough

47. Choose the correct spelling.

a. fictitiuos

b. fictitious

c. fictictious

d. fictititous

48. Choose the correct spelling.

a. partiscular

b. particuler

c. partticular

d. particular

49. Choose the correct spelling.

a. experinment

b. experiment

c. expirement

d. ecperiment

50. Choose the correct spelling.

a. disappereance

b. disapperance

c. disappearance

d. disapearance

Revise these sentences to have better form and grammar.

51. When I was a child, my mother taught me to say thank you, holding the door open for other, and cover my mouth when yawning or coughing.

a. When I was a child, my mother teaching me to say thank you, to hold the door open for others, and cover my mouth when yawning or coughing.

b. When I was a child, my mother taught me say thank you, to hold the door open for others, and to covering my mouth when yawning or coughing.

c. When I was a child, my mother taught me saying thank you, holding the door open for others, and to cover my mouth when yawning or coughing.

d. When I was a child, my mother taught me to say thank you, hold the door open for others, and cover my mouth when yawning or coughing.

52. Mother is talking to a man that wants to hire her to be a receptionist.

a. Mother is talking to a man who wants to hire her to be a receptionist.

b. Mother is talked to a man who wants to hire her to be a receptionist.

c. Mother is talking to a man who wants to her. To be a receptionist.

d. Mother is talking to a man hiring her who to be a receptionist.

53. Those comic books, which was for sale at the magazine shop, are now quite valuable.

a. Those comics books which were for sale, at the magazine shop are now quite valuable.

b. Those comic books, which were for sale at the magazine, shop, are now quite valuable.

c. Those comic books, which were for sale at the magazine shop, are now, quite valuable

d. Those comic books, which were for sale at the magazine shop, are now quite valuable.

Practice Test Questions 2 205

54. If you want to sell your car, it's important being honest with the buyer.

a. If you want to sell your car, being honest with the buyer is important.

b. If you want to sell your car, its important to be honest with the buyer.

c. If you wanting to sell your car, being honest with the buyer are important.

d. If you want to selling your car, to be honest with the buyer is important.

55. Although today the boy was nice to my brother, they usually was quite mean to him.

a. Although today the boy was nice to my brother, they were usually quite mean to him.

b. Although today the boy was nice to my brother, he was usually quite mean to him.

c. Although today the boy was nice to my brother, he is usually quite mean to him.

d. Although today the boy was nice to my brother, he were usually quite mean to him.

Combine the separate sentences into one simpler sentence with the same meaning.

56. The customers were impatient for the store to open. The customers rushed inside as soon as the doors were open.

a. Although the customers were impatient for the store to open, the doors were opened as soon as the customers rushed inside.

b. Although the doors were opened before customers rushed inside, the customers were impatient for the store to open.

c. The customers, who were impatient for the store to open, rushed inside as soon as the doors were open.

d. Although the doors were opened by impatient customers, they rushed inside before the store was open.

57. I should enter my dog in a dog pageant. Everyone says that my dog, whose name is Skipper, is the most beautiful one they've ever seen."

a. Because my dog's name is Skipper, my dog was entered in the pageant and everyone said he was the mot beautiful dog that they've ever seen.

b. I should enter my dog in a dog pageant, since everyone says that Skipper is the most beautiful dog they've ever seen.

c. Before I entered my dog in the dog pageant, Skipper said that he was the most beautiful dog that he'd ever seen.

d. Skipper entered my dog in the dog pageant because he was the most beautiful one that anyone had ever seen.

58. The doctor was not looking forward to meeting Mrs. Lucas. The doctor would have to tell Mrs. Lucas that she has cancer. The doctor hates giving bad news to patients.

a. The doctor hates giving bad news, and so he was not looking forward to meeting Mrs. Lucas because he would have to tell her that she has cancer.

b. The doctor has cancer and was not looking forward to meeting Mrs. Lucas and telling her this bad news.

c. Before the doctor met Mrs. Lucas, he had to give his the patients the bad news that Mrs. Lucas has cancer.

d. The doctor was not looking forward to giving the bad news to his patients that he had to tell Mrs. Lucas that his patients have cancer.

59. Mom hates shopping. We were out of bread, milk and eggs. Mom went to the supermarket.

a. Because we were out of bread, milk and eggs, Mom hated shopping at the supermarket.

b. Although she hates shopping, Mom went to the supermarket since we were out of bread, milk and eggs.

c. Although we were out of bread, milk and eggs, Mom still hated shopping at the supermarket and went there anyway.

d. Because Mom hated shopping at the supermarket, she went to there to buy her bread, milk and eggs.

60. I hate needles. I want to give blood. I can't give blood.

    a. Although I hate needles, I couldn't give blood even if I wanted to.

    b. Because I hate needles, I can't give blood, although I want to give blood.

    c. Whenever I hate needles, I give blood although I can't give blood.

    d. Whenever I can't give blood, I give blood anyway, although I hate needles.

Answer Key

Section I - Verbal Skills

1. D
This is a place relationship. Acting is done in a theater in the same way gambling is done in a casino.

2. C
Pork is the meat of a pig in the same way beef is the meat of a cow.

3. A
This is a classification relationship. The first is the class which the second belongs.

4. C
Slumber is a synonym for sleep and bog is a synonym for swamp.

5. D
This is a part-to-whole relationship. A petal is to a flower as fur is to a rabbit.

6. A
A present celebrates a birthday and a reward celebrates an accomplishment.

7. C
This is a functional relationship. A shovel is used to dig and scissors are used to snip.

8. A
This is a parts-to-whole relationship. The finger is part of the hand in the same way, a leg is part of a body.

9. B
The first is the study of the second. Zoology is the study of animals in the same way botany is the study of plants.

10. B
This is a type relationship. A child is a young human just as a kitten is a young cat.

11. B
This is a composition relationship. A candle is made of wax and a bowl is made of clay.

12. B
Able and competent are synonyms.

13. A
Antidote and cure are synonyms.

14. C
Consensus and agreement are synonyms.

15. A
Magnify and amplify are synonyms.

16. B
Immaculate and perfect are synonyms.

17. C
Feasible and viable are synonyms.

18. B
Reason and rationale are synonyms.

19. A
Tinge and touch are synonyms.

20. C
Gist and summary are synonyms.

21. C
Initiate and instigate are synonyms.

22. A
Expertise and specialty are synonyms.

23. B
Amazing and extraordinary are synonyms.

24. C
Furious and angry are synonyms.
25. A
Inquire and ask are synonyms.

26. A
Awful and terrible are synonyms.

27. C
Wicked and evil are synonyms.

28. False
You cannot real a negative conclusion from 2 positive statements.

29. Uncertain

No information is given about houses NOT on Appleby or Francisco streets.

30. Uncertain

It is possible that some of my tropical fish are very sensitive, but it is also possible that they are all insensitive varieties.

31. Uncertain

I may be rich or I may not be.

32. False

IF Science can explain all events, AND making a decision is an event, THEN science CAN explain how I make a decision.

33. False.

There are 2 problems. Doctors can sometimes predict epidemics. Bird Flu is becoming an epidemic.

Bird flu is not an epidemic yet, and doctors can only predict epidemics sometimes.

34. Uncertain.

My textbook MAY have come from that store or it may have come from another store.

35. D

This is a relationship of words question. All the choices are dinnerware except dinner.

36. A

This is a relationship of words question. All the choices are major planets except the moon.

37. D

This is a relationship of words question. All the choices are cat or feline family except fox.

38. B

This is a relationship of words question. All the choices are plants, except garden.

39. B

This is a relationship of words question. All the choices are related to lawn except flowers.

40. A

This is a synonym relationship. Influential has the same meaning as powerful.

Practice Test Questions 2

41. D
This is an antonym relationship. Careful is the opposite meaning of reckless.

42. C
This is an opposite relationship. Prey is the opposite meaning of predator.

43. A
This is a synonym relationship. Shimmer has the same meaning as sheen.

44. C
This is a synonym relationship. Foe has the same meaning as enemy.

45. D
This is a synonym relationship. Unconventional has the same meaning as off-beat.

46. A
This is a classification relationship. Frogs are amphibians, and snakes are reptiles.

47. C
Red is a color and triangle is a shape.

48. C
Skirt is a type of clothing as Mars is a planet.

49. C
Intelligent has the same relation to brilliant as fat to obese.

50. B
Busted has the same relation to broken as bland to plain.

51. A
Occupation has the same relation to work as two to binary.

52. C
A zoologist studies animals, and a botanist studies plants.

53. B
Fixed and indefinite are antonyms.

54. C
Strategic and unplanned are antonyms.

55. B
Authentic and imitation are antonyms.

56. D
Villian and hero are antonyms.

57. A
Vanish and appear are antonyms.

58. C
Literal and figurative are antonyms.

59. A
Harsh and mild are antonyms.

60. D
Splurge and save are antonyms.

Section II – Quantitative Skills

1. D
The sequence is increasing. Each new term is obtained by multiplying the last term by 2. Therefore, 80 x 2 = 160

2. C
Each new term is calculated by subtracting 100 from the last term. So, 18095 – 100 = 17995

3. B
Each new term is calculated by adding 6 to the last term, therefore, -27 + 6 = -21

4. C
The sequence increases initially and then decreases in the next term. The relationship between each increase is +200 and the relationship with the alternate decrease is -300. So the answer is -300 + 200 = -100

5. B
The sequence is increasing. Each new term is derived by multiplying the last term with an increasing number. The first term is multiplied by 1 to get the next term. That is multiplied by 2 to get the 3rd term, which is multiplied by 3 to get the 4th term. So the answer is 12.18 x 4 = 48.72

6. D
This sequence is increasing. The sequence increases by multiplying by 3 and adding 3. The first term the sequence is increasing by multiplying and adding 3 alternatively. The first term was multiplied by 3 to get the second term, and that was added to 3. The answer = 36 x 3 = 108

Practice Test Questions 2

7. B

The sequence increases and decreases alternatively. The rate of increase is +2 and decrease is -3, so the answer = 346 – 3 = 343

8. A

The sequence is increase after repeating the last term. The answer = 41 + 10 = 51

9. A

The first two terms increased by +3. The difference between each subsequent term is the rate of last increase + 2. So answer is 29 + 7 + 2 = 38

10. B

First two terms decreased by 11 and the subsequent terms decreased by subtracting 2 from the last rate of decrease. Answer is 7 – (5-2) = 7-3 =4.

11. D

The sequence is increasing by adding 2 and multiplying 2 alternatively. The next 2 terms are 24 + 2= 26 and 26 x 2 = 52.

12. C

The sequence is decreasing by 8.

13. B

The sequence is increasing by multiplying the last term by 3. 2.7 x 3= 8.1 and 8.1 x 3 = 24.3

14. A

The sequence is decreasing by dividing the last term by 2.

15. C

The sequence is increasing by 7.

16. C

The sequence is increasing by 3.

17. B

The sequence is decreasing by 5.

18. C

The sequence is decreasing by -5 and -10 alternatively the first term is 75 – 5 = 70 and the last term is 35 – 5 = 30.

19. C
20. B
21. A
22. B
23. A
24. B

25. C
26. A
27. B

28. B
#1 = 48
#2 = 58
#3 = 84
3 is greater than 1

29. B
#1 = 42
#2 = 60
#3 = 25
1 < 2 > 3

30. A
#1 = 30
#2 = 64
#3 = 37
1 < 3 < 2

31. B
#1 = 17
#2 = 40
#3 = 47
1 < 3 > 2

32. A
#1 = 20
#2 = 105
#3 = 30
3 < 2 > 1

33. B
#1 = 252
#2 = 350
#3 = 60
2 > 1 > 3

34. B
#1 = 27
#2 = 2
#3 = 22
2 < 1 > 3

35. D
#1 = 90
#2 = 185
#3 = 48
3 < 1 < 2

36. B
#1 = 19
#2 = 13
#3 = 7
1 and 3 are not equal

37. B
$(2/3)Z + 10 = 3 \times 15$
$2/3\ Z = 45 - 10$
$Z = 35 \times 3/2$
$Z = 52.5$

38. A
$X = 25 + (1/3 * 27)$
$X = 25 + 9$
$X = 34$

39. C
$Z = (5 \times 5) - 10$
$Z = 15$

40. A
$3/4 \times 40 = 30 + 12 = 42$

41. C
30% of $120 = 40 + 25 = 65$

42. B
$75 - x = 15 + (3/5 * 75)$
$75 - x = 45 + 15$
$75 - x = 60$
$x = 75 - 60 = 15$

43. A
2/3 of $100 = 66.66 \times 5 = 333.33$

44. C
$9 \times 5 = 45 \times 2 = 90$

45. B
$58 - 10 = 48 \div 8 = 6$

Practice Test Questions 2   217

46. B
1/5 of 40 = 8
25 – X = 8
X = 17

47. C
1/4 of 16 = 4
4 – 1 = 3

48. C
8 X 7 = 56 X 2 = 112

49. A
65 - 15 = 50 ÷ 10 = 5

50. B
1/5 of 60 = 12
25 – X = 12
X = 13

Section III – Reading

1. B
We can infer an important part of the respiratory system are the lungs. From the passage, "Molecules of oxygen and carbon dioxide are passively exchanged, by diffusion, between the gaseous external environment and the blood. This process occurs in the alveolar region of the lungs."

Therefore, a primary function for the respiratory system is the exchange of oxygen and carbon dioxide, and this process occurs in the lungs. We can therefore infer that the lungs are an important part of the respiratory system.

2. C
The process by which molecules of oxygen and carbon dioxide are passively exchanged is diffusion.

This is a definition type question. Scan the passage for references to "oxygen," "carbon dioxide," or "exchanged."

3. A
The organ that plays an important role in gas exchange in amphibians is the skin.

Scan the passage for references to "amphibians," and find the answer.

4. A
The three physiological zones of the respiratory system are Conducting, transitional, respiratory zones.

5. B

This warranty does not cover a product that you have tried to fix yourself. From paragraph two, "This limited warranty does not cover ... any unauthorized disassembly, repair, or modification. "

6. C

ABC Electric could either replace or repair the fan, provided the other conditions are met. ABC Electric has the option to repair or replace.

7. B

The warranty does not cover a stove damaged in a flood. From the passage, "This limited warranty does not cover any damage to the product from improper installation, accident, abuse, misuse, natural disaster, insufficient or excessive electrical supply, abnormal mechanical or environmental conditions."

A flood is an "abnormal environmental condition," and a natural disaster, so it is not covered.

8. A

A missing part is an example of defective workmanship. This is an error made in the manufacturing process. A defective part is not considered workmanship.

9. B

The first paragraph tells us that myths are a true account of the remote past.

The second paragraph tells us that, "myths generally take place during a primordial age, when the world was still young, before achieving its current form."

Putting these two together, we can infer that humankind used myth to explain how the world was created.

10. A

This passage is about different types of stories. First, the passage explains myths, and then compares other types of stories to myths.

11. B

Folktales are different to myths, in that, "Unlike myths, folktales can take place at any time and any place, and the natives do not usually consider them true or sacred."

12. B

This passage describes the different categories for traditional stories. The other choices are facts from the passage, not the main idea of the passage. The main idea of a passage will always be the most general statement. For example, choice A, Myths, fables, and folktales are not the same thing, and each describes a specific type of story. This is a true statement from the passage, but not the main idea of the passage, since the passage also talks about how some cultures may classify a story as a myth and others as a folktale.

The statement, from choice B, Traditional stories can be categorized in different ways by different people, is a more general statement that describes the passage.

13. B

Choice B is the best choice, categories that group traditional stories according to certain characteristics.

Choices A and C are false and can be eliminated right away. Choice D is designed to confuse. Choice D may be true, but it is not mentioned in the passage.

14. D

The best answer is D, traditional stories themselves are a part of the larger category of folklore, which may also include costumes, gestures, and music.

All the other choices are false. Traditional stories are part of the larger category of folklore, which includes other things, not the other way around.

15. A

This passage shows there is a distinct difference between a myth and a legend, although both are folktales.

16. D

This question tests the reader's summarization skills. The question is asking very generally about the message of the passage, and the title, "Ways Characters Communicate in Theater," is one indication of that. The other answers A, B, and C are all directly from the text, and therefore readers may be inclined to select one of them, but are too specific to encapsulate the entirety of the passage and its message.

17. B

The paragraph on soliloquies mentions "To be or not to be," and it is from the context of that paragraph that readers may understand that because "To be or not to be" is a soliloquy, Hamlet will be introspective, or thoughtful, while delivering it. It is true that actors deliver soliloquies alone, and may be "solitary" (A), but "thoughtful" (B) is more true to the overall idea of the paragraph. Readers may choose C because drama and theater can be used interchangeably and the passage mentions that soliloquies are unique to theater (and therefore drama), but this answer is not specific enough to the paragraph in question. Readers may pick up on the theme of life and death and Hamlet's true intentions and select that he is "hopeless" (D), but those themes are not discussed either by this paragraph or passage, as a close textual reading and analysis confirms.

18. C

This question tests the reader's grammatical skills. B seems logical, but parenthesis are actually considered to be a stronger break in a sentence than commas are, and along this line of thinking, actually disrupt the sentence more. A and D make comparisons between theater and film that are simply not made in the passage, and may or may not be true. This detail does clarify the statement that asides are most unique to theater by adding that it is not completely unique to theater, which may have been why the author didn't chose not to delete it and instead used parentheses to designate the detail's importance (C).

19. C
This question tests the reader's vocabulary and contextualization skills. A may or may not be true, but focuses on the wrong function of the word "give" and ignores the rest of the sentence, which is more relevant to what the passage is discussing. B and D may also be selected if the reader depends too literally on the word "give," failing to grasp the more abstract function of the word that is the focus of answer C, which also properly acknowledges the entirety of the passage and its meaning.

20. B
The inference is botanists have not surveyed all the tropical areas so they do not know the number of species. Species diversity here refers to the number of species.

21. A
Most species grow in tropical regions. This is taken directly from the passage.

22. D
Tree-ferns survived the Carboniferous period. This is a fact-based question about the Carboniferous period. "Carboniferous" is an unusual word, so the fastest way to answer this question is to scan the pas-sage for the word "Carboniferous" and find the answer.

23. B
Here is the passage with the oldest to youngest trees.

The earliest trees were [1] tree ferns and horsetails, which grew in forests in the Carboniferous period. Tree ferns still survive, but the only surviving horsetails are no longer in tree form. Later, in the Triassic period, [2] conifers and ginkgos, appeared, [3] followed by flowering plants after that in the Cretaceous period.

24. B
The time limit for radar detectors is 14 days. Since you made the purchase 15 days ago, you do not qualify for the guarantee.

25. B
Since you made the purchase 10 days ago, you are covered by the guarantee. Since it is an advertised price at a different store, ABC Electric will "beat" the price by 10% of the difference, which is,

500 – 400 = 100 – difference in price

100 X 10% = $10 – 10% of the difference

The advertised lower price is $400. ABC will beat this price by 10% so they will refund $100 + 10 = $110.

26. C
The purpose of this passage is to persuade.

27. B
Insects have 3 units, not to be confused with segments. From the first paragraph, "The segments of the body are organized into three distinctive connected units, a head, a thorax, and an abdomen."

This question tries to confuse 'segments' and 'units.'

28. D
This question tries to confuse. Read the passage carefully to find reference to the number of wings. "...if present in the species, two or four wings."

From this, we can conclude some insects have no wings, (if present ...) some have 2 wings, and some have 4 wings. Choice D does not mention insects that don't have wings, but it is still the best choice of the choices given.

29. A
The question asks about the abdomen and choices refer to organs in the abdomen. The passage says, "The abdomen also contains most of the digestive, respiratory, ... "

The choices are,

> a. It contains some of the organs.
>
> b. It is too small for any organs.
>
> c. It contains all of the organs.
>
> d. None of the above.

Choice A is true, but we need to see if there is better choice before answering. Choice B is not true. Choice C is not true since the relevant sentence says 'most' not 'all.' Choice D can be eliminated since Choice A is true.

Given there is not better choice, Choice A is the best choice answer.

30. D
This question tests the reader's summarization skills. The other answers A, B, and C focus on portions of the second paragraph that are too narrow and do not relate to the specific portion of text in question. The complexity of the sentence may mislead students into selecting one of these answers, but rearranging or restating the sentence will lead the reader to the correct answer. In addition, A makes an assumption that may or may not be true about the intentions of the company, B focuses on one product rather than the idea of the products, and C makes an assumption about women that may or may not be true and is not sup-

ported by the text.

31. B
This question tests reader's attention to detail. If a reader selects A, he or she may have picked up on the use of the word "debate" and assumed, very logically, that the two are at odds because they are fighting; however, this is simply not supported in the text. C also uses very specific quotes from the text, but it rearranges them and gives them false meaning. The artists want to elevate their creations above the creations of other artists, thereby showing that they are "creative" and "innovative." Similarly, D takes phrases straight from the texts and rearranges and confuses them. The artists are described as wanting to be "creative, innovative, individual people," not the women.

32. A
This question tests reader's vocabulary and summarization skills. This phrase, used by the author, may seem flippant and dismissive if readers focus on the word "whatever" and misinterpret it as a popular, colloquial terms. In this way, the answers B and C may mislead the reader to selecting one of them by including the terms "unimportant" and "stupid," respectively. D is a similar misreading, but doesn't make sense when the phrase is at the beginning of the passage and the entire passage is on media messages. A is literarily and contextually appropriate, and the reader can understand that the author would like to keep the introduction focused on the topic the passage is going to discuss.

33. A
This question tests a reader's inference skills. The extreme use of the word "all" in B suggests that every single advertising company are working to be approachable, and while this is not only unlikely, the text specifically states that "more" companies have done this, signifying that they have not all participated, even if it's a possibility that they may some day. The use of the limiting word "only" in C lends that answer similar problems; women are still buying from companies who do not care about this message, or those companies would not be in business, and the passage specifies that "many" women are worried about media messages, but not all. Readers may find D logical, especially if they are looking to make an inference, and while this may be a possibility, the passage does not suggest or discuss this happening. A is correct based on specifically because of the relation between "still working" in the answer and "will hopefully" and the extensive discussion on companies struggles, which come only with progress, in the text.

34. C
This question tests the reader's summarization skills. The entire passage is leading up to the idea that the president of the US may not have had grounds to assert his Fourteen Points when other countries had lost so much. A is pretty directly inferred by the text, but it does not adequately summarize what the entire passage is trying to communicate. B may also be inferred by the passage when it says that the war is "imminent," but it does not represent the entire message, either. The passage does seem to be in praise of FDR, or at least in respect of

him, but it does not in any way claim that he is the smartest president, nor does this represent the many other points included. C is then the obvious answer, and most directly relates to the closing sentences which it rewords.

35. C

This question tests the reader's attention to detail. The passage does state that A and B are true, and while those statements are in proximity to the explanation for why the war started, they are not the actual reason given. D is a mix up of words used in the passage, which says that the largest powers were in play but not that this fact somehow started the war. The passage does make a direct statement that a domino effect started the war, supporting C as the correct answer.

36. A

This question tests the reader's understanding of functions in writing. Through-out the passage, it states that leaders of other nations were hesitant to accept generous or peaceful terms because of the grievances of the war, and the great loss of life was chief among these. While the passage does touch on the devastation of deadly weapons (B), the use of this raw, emotional fact serves a much larger purpose, and the focus of the passage is not the weapons. While readers may indeed consider who lost the most soldiers (C) when so many countries were involved and the inequalities of loss are mentioned in the passage, there is no discussion of this in the passage. D is related to A, But A is more direct and relates more to the passage.

37. B

This question tests the reader's vocabulary skills. A may seem appealing to readers because it is phonetically similar to "catalyzed," but the two are not related in any other way. C makes sense in context, but if plugged in to the sentence creates a redundancy that doesn't make sense. D does also not make sense contextually, even if the reader may consider that funds were needed to create more weaponry, especially if it was advanced.

Section IV - Vocabulary

38. A
Anecdote: n. A short account of an incident

39. B
Heinous: adj. shocking, terrible or
wicked.

40. A
Harbinger: n. a person of thing that tells or announces the coming of someone or something

41. B
Judicious: Having, or characterized by, good judgment or sound thinking.

42. B
Ethanol: n. a colorless volatile flammable liquid C2H6O.

43. A
Respiratory: adj. Of, relating to, or affecting respiration or the organs of respiration.

44. B
Inherent: Naturally a part or consequence of something.

45. A
Vapid: adj. tasteless or bland.

46. C
Waif: n. homeless child or stray.

47. D
Homologous: adj. similar or identical.

48. B
Obsolete: adj. no longer in use; gone into disuse; disused or neglected.
49. A
Rankle: v. To cause irritation or deep bitterness.

50. C
Renewable

51. C
Torpid: adj. Lazy, lethargic or apathetic.

52. A
Gregarious: adj. Describing one who enjoys being in crowds and socializing.

53. B
Mutation: n. a change or alteration.

54. C
Lithe: adj. flexible or pliant.

55. A
Resent: v. to express displeasure or indignation.

56. A
Immaterial: adj. irrelevant not having substance or matter.

57. A
Impeccable: adj. perfect, no faults or errors.

58. B
Pudgy: adj. fat, plump or overweight.

59. C
Alloy: v. Mix or combine; often used of metals.

60. B
Combustible: adj. Able to catch fire and burn easily.

Section V – Math

1. B
Let XY represent the initial number, X + Y = 12, YX=XY+ 36, only b = 48 satisfies both equations.

2. A
The problem is to find the perimeter of a shape made by merging a square and a semi circle. Perimeter = 3 sides of the square + 1/2 circumference of the circle.
= (3 x 5) + ½(5 π)
= 15 + 2.5 π
Perimeter = 17.5 π cm

3. B
Let the father's age=Y, and Kate's age = X, therefore Y = 32 + X, in 5 years y = 5x, substituting for Y will be 5x = 32 + X, 5x – x = 32, 4X = 32,X = 32/8, x = 8, Kate will be 8 in 5 years time, so Kate's present age = 8 - 5 = 3.

4. A
This is a simple direct proportion problem:
If Lynn can type 1 page in p minutes,

she can type x pages in 5 minutes

We do cross multiplication: x•p = 5•1

Then,

x = 5/p

5. A
This is an inverse ration problem.

1/x = 1/a + 1/b where a is the time Sally can paint a house, b is the time John can paint a house, x is the time Sally and John can together paint a house.

So,

1/x = 1/4 + 1/6 ... We use the least common multiple in the denominator that is 24:

1/x = 6/24 + 4/24

1/x = 10/24

x = 24/10

x = 2.4 hours.

In other words; 2 hours + 0.4 hours = 2 hours + 0.4•60 minutes

= 2 hours 24 minutes

6. D
First add all the numbers 62 + 18 + 39 + 13 + 16 + 37 + 25 = 210. Then divide by 7 (the number of data provided) = 210/7 = 30

7. B
Last season's ticket = X,
X + (10/100)X = 880
100x + 10x = 88000
110x = 88000
x = 88000/110
x = 800

8. B
Total Volume = Volume of large cylinder - Volume of small cylinder

Volume of a cylinder = area of base • height = πr^2•h

Total Volume = (π•122•10) - (π•62•5) = 1440π - 180π

= 1260π in^3

9. A
Distance traveled by 1st train in 20 minutes = (72 km/hr × 20 minutes) /60 minutes = 24 km. Distance traveled by 2nd train in 20 minutes = (52 km/hr × 20 minutes)/60 minutes = 17.33 km. Since the trains are travelling in opposite directions, add the distances for the difference apart, 24 + 17.33 = 41.33 km.

10. B
Suppose oranges in the basket before = x
Then according to the condition
X + 8x/5 = 130
5x + 8x = 650
X = 50

11. D
We have a circle given with diameter 8 cm and a square located within the circle. We are asked to find the area of the circle for which we only need to know the length of the radius that is the half of the diameter.

Area of circle = πr^2 ... r = 8/2 = 4 cm

Area of circle = $\pi * 4^2$

= 16π cm^2 ... As we notice, the inner square has no role in this question.

12. C
In one trip around the track, he covers the distance equal to the circumference of the circular path.
Circumference of the path=75×π=235.65 meters.
Distance covered in 7 rounds=235.65×7=1650 meters.

13. B
This is an inverse proportion question. The number of employees decreases then working time will increase.

Employees	Working hours
12	7
10	x

Therefore, the equation will be
x/7 = 12/10
x = 7 * 12/10
x = 7.2

Therefore, the remaining staff will have to work, in minutes, 0.2 × 60 = 12 minutes.

14. B
The speed is 300km/hr so it will cover 5 km/minute. Therefore, the train will travel 45km in 9 minutes. Time to arrive at station B will be 9:05 pm.

15. A
The angles opposite both angles 30° & angle d are respectively equal to vertical angles.
$2(30° + d) = 360°$
$2d = 360° - 60°$
$2d = 300°$
$d = 150°$

16. A
George's average speed = 80/32/ = 25 km/hr.
Average speed for Marsha is 23 km/hr.
The distance covered by Marsha in 3.2 hrs = 3.2 X 23 = 73.6 km

So Marsha will be 80 – 73.6 = 6.4 km away from the finish when George crosses.

17. C
The length of the track = 1.2 km = 1200 meters.
John will complete 1 round in 1200/120 = 10 minutes.
Tony will complete 1 round in 1200/100 = 12 minutes.
David will complete 1 round in 1200/75 = 16 minutes.
The Least Common Multiple of these is 240. Therefore, they will be together after 240 minutes.

18. D
As 1 cm = 5 km so 12.4 cm will be = 12.4×5=62 km

19. C
Number of problems remaining = 40 – 28 = 12
Time remaining = 30 – 25 = 5 minutes = 5 X 60 = 300 seconds. Time for each remaining question = 300/12 = 25 seconds.

20. B
Perimeter of a parallelogram is the sum of the sides.

Perimeter = 2(l+b)
Perimeter = 2(3+10), 2 x 13
Perimeter = 26 cm

21. D
2009 X 108 is approximately 210,000. The actual number is 216,972.

22. A
The purchase price of 12 shirts when profit is 8% = 0.92 X 336 = $309.12 The

purchase price of each shirt = 309.12/12 = $25.76

23. C
This is a proportionality question.
12 : 4
X : 20

4 * 5 = 20 and 12 * 5 = X
X = 60

24. D
First, convert everything to seconds.
Song A = 240 + 56 = 296 sec.
Song B = 120 + 30 = 150 sec.
Song C = 600 + 16 = 616 sec.
Total = 296 + 150 + 616 = 1062. Average will be 1062/3 = 354.
In hours, 354/60 = 5 minutes, 54 seconds.

25. B
8.50 * .4 = 3.40 + 1.30 = $4.70

26. D
We can determine the price of single rooms from the information given for the
second company. 13 single rooms = 3185.

One single room = 3185 / 13 = 245
The first company paid for 6 single rooms at $245. 245 x 6 = $1470

Total amount paid for 4 double rooms by first company = $2850 - $1470 = $1380
Cost per double room = 1380 / 4 = $345

27. B
Formula for perimeter of a rectangle is 2(L + W)
p=26, so 2(L+W) = p

The length is 5 inches more than the width, so
2(w+5) + 2w = 26
2w + 10 + 2w = 26
2w + 2w = 26 - 10
4w = 18
W = 16/4 = 4 inches
L is 5 inches more than w, so L = 5 + 4 = 9 inches.

28. A
Number of mangos in the basket is 3/5 x 125 = 75
Number of ripe mangos = 2/5 x 75 = 30

29. D
Substitute the known variables, (3 x 2) + (4 x 4) x 8 =, 6 + 16 x 8, 24 x 8 = 176

30. A
2cnx = 2(4 x 5 x 3)/(2 X 5) =, 2 x 60/2 x 5 =, 120/10 = 12

31. A
First change all the terms to fractions, therefore, we get 7/2 / 14/5, to divide we
need to invert the second fraction, 7/2 x 5/14, and then we cancel out to reduce
to the lowest terms, 1/2 x 5/2 = 5/4, convert back to proper fraction to get 1 1/4

32. B
Substitute known variables, 2 x 9/3 + 3 x 10/5 – 2 =, 18/3 + 30/5 – 2
(6 + 6) - 2
12 - 2 = 10

33. A
First solve the fraction in each bracket separately, therefore (1/3 + 2/6) - (3/4
- 1/3) = (find common denominator) (2+2/6) – (9- 4/12) = (4/6) – (5/12) = (find
common denominator again) 2/3 – 5/12 =, 8 - 5/12 = 3/12 = 1/4.

34. B
(4/5 - 3/10) + (2/3 – 3/9) =, (find a common denominator) (8-3/10) + (6-3/9) =,
(5/10) + (3/9) = 2/5 + 1/3, (find a common denominator) 6+5/15 = 11/15

35. A
2 + a number divided by 7.
(2 + X) divided by 7.
(2 + X)/7

36. D
Substitute with known variables, (6 x 8) – 12 + (2 x 12) =, 48 – 12 + 24, do the ad-
ditions first, 48 – (12 + 24) =, 48 – 36 = 12

37. C
Subtract the whole numbers and then subtract the fractions, therefore 3 2/3 - 1
2/8 = (3-1) (2/3 – 2/8) = find common denominator to subtract the fractions, (2)
(16-6)/24 = 2 10/24, reduce to lowest terms, 2 5/12

38. A
Subtract the whole numbers and then subtract the fractions, therefore (7-4) (2/5
– 3/10) = 3 (4-3/10) = 3 1/10

39. C

-4 – 5x = 8x + 8, bring same terms to same side of the equation changing the negative or positive signs when they cross over, therefore -5x + 8x = 8 + 4, = 3x = 12, x = 12/3, x = 4.

40. A

First, convert all the terms to fractions and then cancel out. Therefore, 7/3 x 10/7 x 3/4 = 1/3 x 10/1 x 3/4, 1/3 x 5/1 x 3/2, 1/3 x 5/1 x 3/2 = 15/6 = 2 1/2

41. B

Subtract the whole numbers and then subtract the fractions, therefore (7 - 4) (4/5 – 2/3) = 3 (12 - 10/15) = 3 2/15

42. C

12x – 8 = 3x + 10, bring same terms to same side of the equation changing the negative or positive signs when they cross over, therefore 12x - 3x = 10 + 8, 9x = 18, x = 2

43. C

(3/5 - 2/5) + (3/4 – 2/8) =, (3-2/5) + (6-2/8) =, 1/5 + 2/8 =, (find a common denominator) 8+10/40 = 18/40

44. D

6a + 4 = 28 + 2a, then a = , bring same terms to same side of the equation changing the negative or positive signs when they cross over, therefore 6a – 2a = 28 - 4, 4a = 24, a = 24/4 = 6

45. D

(3-1/4) – (3-2/5) =, 3/4 - 1/5 =. 15-4/20 = 11/20

46. D

6 + 9x = 12 + 7x, bring same terms to same side of the equation changing the negative or positive signs when they cross over, therefore 9x – 7x = 12 – 6, 2x = 6, x = 6/2, x = 3

47. C

First change all the terms to fractions, therefore, we get 32/5 / 16/7, to divide we need to invert the second fraction, 32/5 x 7/16, and then we cancel out to reduce to the lowest terms, 2/5 x 7/1 = 14/5, convert back to proper fraction to get 2 4/5

48. B

-6 + 7a = 9 + 4a, bring same terms to same side of the equation changing the negative or positive signs when they cross over, therefore 7a – 4a = 9 + 6 = 3a = 15, a = 15/3, a = 5

49. B

First change all the terms to fractions, therefore, we get 7/3 / 7/5, to divide we need to invert the second fraction, 7/3 x 5/7, and then we cancel out to reduce to the lowest terms, 1/3 x 5/1 = 5/3, convert back to proper fraction to get 1 2/3

50. B
First, convert all the terms to fractions and then cancel out. Therefore, 2/3 x 11/7 x 21/4 = 2/3 x 11/1 x 3/4, 1/3 x 11/1 x 3/2, 1/1 x 11/1 x 1/2 = 11/2 = 5 1/2

51. A
First change all the terms to fractions, therefore, we get 21/5 / 7/3, to divide we need to invert the second fraction, 21/5 x 3/7, and then we cancel out to reduce to the lowest terms, 3/5 x 3/1 = 9/5, convert back to proper fraction to get 1 4/5

52. B
First, convert all the terms to fractions and then cancel out. Therefore, 10/3 x 9/4 x 16/5 = 10/1 x 3/4 x 16/5, 10/1 x 3/1 x 4/5, 2/1 x 3/1 x 4/1 = 24/1 = 24

53. C
First change all the terms to fractions, therefore, we get 28/9 / 8/3, to divide we need to invert the second fraction, 28/9 x 3/8, and then we cancel out to reduce to the lowest terms, 28/9 X 3/8 = 28/3 X 1/8 = 28/24 = 14/12 = 7/6, convert back to proper fraction to get 1 1/6

54. C
+(+) becomes a positive sign and -(-) equals +, therefore -9 + (+6) – (-2) = -9 + 6 + 2 = -3 + 2 = -1

55. B
(5-5) (1/2 – 3/7) = (7-6/14) = 1/14

56. D
-(-) becomes + and -(+) becomes -, therefore, -3 - (-7) - (+5) = -3 + 7 – 5, 4 - 5 = -1

57. D
First, convert all the terms to fractions and then cancel out. Therefore, 15/4 x 4/5 x 7/4 = 3/4 x 4/1 x 7/4, 3/4 x 1/1 x 7/1, 21/4 = 5 1/4

58. A
(6 - 4) (3/5 – 4/5) = 2 (3 - 4/5) = since 3 is less than 4, we would have to subtract 1 from the whole number besides the fraction, therefore 1 13 - 4/5 = 1 9/5 = 2 4/5

59. B
46,227 + 101,032 = 147.259, or approximately 147,000.

60. A
$\sqrt{121} = 11$

Section V – Language Arts

1. D
A colon informs the reader that what follows the mark proves, explains, or lists elements of what preceded the mark.

2. D
A colon informs the reader that what follows the mark proves, explains, or lists elements of what preceded the mark.

3. C
The dash is used when the speaker cannot continue.

4. B
The dash is used to indicate a closed range of values.

5. A
Do not use a period after Roman numerals.

6. A
A period should be used for academic degrees when abbreviated. In choice B, it should be B.S.N. For choices C and D, do not use a period for abbreviations that are accepted as the shortened form of proper names like National Aeronautics and Space Administration (NASA), and Federal Bureau of Investigation (FBI).

7. C
A period is used to end an imperative sentence, that is, at the end of a direction or a command.

8. A
North, South, East, and West are only capitalized when used as sections of the country, but not as compass directions.

9. D
The New York Times is the name of a publication so capitalized. Mottos, slogans and notices are capitalized. For example, Employees Only, or All the News That's Fit to Print.

10. B
President is not capitalized unless used with a name as in, President Obama.

11. C
The names of plays are capitalized. All words except articles are capitalized.

12. C

Made in the USA
San Bernardino, CA
21 January 2017